ALCOHOL RECOVERY BOOKS

Master Your Brain to Obtain Freedom From Alcoholism

(Alcohol Addiction Guide to Overcoming Alcohol Addiction)

Rickie Franco

Published by Tomas Edwards

© **Rickie Franco**

All Rights Reserved

Alcohol Recovery Books: Master Your Brain to Obtain Freedom From Alcoholism (Alcohol Addiction Guide to Overcoming Alcohol Addiction)

ISBN 978-1-990373-33-6

Legal & Disclaimer

The information contained in this book is not designed to replace or take the place of any form of medicine or professional medical advice. The information in this book has been provided for educational and entertainment purposes only.

The information contained in this book has been compiled from sources deemed reliable, and it is accurate to the best of the Author's knowledge; however, the Author cannot guarantee its accuracy and validity and cannot be held liable for any errors or omissions. Changes are periodically made to this book. You must consult your doctor or get professional medical advice before using any of the suggested remedies, techniques, or information in this book.

Upon using the information contained in this book, you agree to hold harmless the Author from and against any damages, costs, and expenses, including any legal fees potentially resulting from the application of any of the information provided by this guide. 'This disclaimer applies to any damages or injury caused by the use and application, whether directly or indirectly, of any advice or information presented, whether for breach of contract, tort, negligence, personal injury, criminal intent, or under any other cause of action.

You agree to accept all risks of using the information presented inside this book. You need to consult a professional medical practitioner in order to ensure you are both able and healthy enough to participate in this program.

Table of Contents

Introduction

In this book you'll find proven steps and strategies on how to stop drinking alcohol and become independent from its effects once and for all..

This book contains proven strategies to help you break free from alcohol addiction. It also presents techniques to deal with alcohol withdrawal, which is very common in people that are excessive drinkers. All the strategies mentioned here are safe and effective.

It's not always easy to see when your drinking has crossed the line from moderate or social use to problem drinking. But if you consume alcohol to cope with difficulties or to avoid feeling bad, you're in potentially dangerous territory. Alcoholism and alcohol abuse

1

can sneak up on you, so it's important to be aware of the warning signs and take steps to cut back if you recognize them. Understanding the problem is the first step to overcoming it.

Thanks again for downloading this book, I hope you enjoy it!

Chapter 1: Definition Of Alcoholism

There are many definitions of alcoholism. The most common definition of alcoholism is that "alcoholism is a horrible disease that affects the whole person ". However this definition may also apply to cancer or other dreadful diseases. Alcoholism cannot be defined simply as a disease caused by prolonged consumption of alcohol. The amount and frequency of drinking will determine alcoholism.

A more accurate definition of alcoholism suggests a chronic disorder characterized by some loss of control over drinking. Drinking more frequently and at inappropriate times will point towards alcoholism. Alcoholism is a common term for two distinct disorders. They are alcohol abuse and alcohol dependence.

The medical definition of alcoholism describes alcoholism as a disease caused by continuous consumption of alcohol. The quantity and frequency of alcohol consumption required to develop alcoholism will vary from person to person.

Alcoholism is also qualified by some other expressions. They include use, misuse, heavy use, abuse and dependence. Use is a term which simply refers to a person who drinks any alcoholic products. Misuse and heavy use do not have any standard definitions. Heavy use of alcohol will vary from person to person depending upon the age, alcohol brand and so on.

Alcohol abuse is one of the serious problems which lead to poor nutrition, memory loss, difficulty in walking and liver diseases. It will also generate mental stress, depression, fatigue, employment problems, family problems etc. Alcohol abuse may also involve the drinker in legal problems at some point in his life. The drinker will continue to drink at this stage irrespective of his health and family problems.

Addiction to alcohol will cause alcohol dependency. Alcohol dependence will cause social and work related problems. The drinker will experience periods of shaking, sweating and nausea when he tries to stop drinking when he reaches the stage of addiction. Alcohol dependence is usually indicated if the following symptoms are present:

1. Increases in level of tolerance to alcohol.

2. The drinker will take more alcohol to avoid withdrawal symptoms.

3. He will lose control over drinking.

4. He may spend more time in drinking and will recover from it only after long period of time.

5. He will lose interest in social and recreational activities.

6. He will continue to drink though he knows the adverse effects of drinking.

Alcoholism will lead most of the alcoholics to increase their consumption. Loss of control will happen in this stage. In fact loss of control is a clear symptom of alcoholism. As the drinker continues to drink, his body will build increased tolerance towards alcohol. Therefore the drinker will not get fully content by consuming the usual amount of alcohol. He will need more and more. Withdrawal symptoms like nausea, sweating and shaking will also appear.

Alcohol problems will vary from person to person. The severity of alcoholism will also vary from drinker to drinker. Some may experience life threatening problems. Liver dysfunction, brain disorders etc will also occur. Rightly said, alcoholism is a horrible disease. However it is possible to cure the disease. Alcoholics Anonymous have helped millions through their method of sharing their experiences amongst themselves as long as the member desires to stop drinking. Health Coaching is another method in which the alcoholic recognizes the effects of his behavior on his body, his family and his surroundings and obtains personalized help to take action and continue his sobriety.

DEFINITION OF ALCOHOLISM - RELEVANT OR NOT?

With many different opinions and approaches it is not easy to give a definition of alcoholism. Definitions in general often evoke contrasting views which can be rather confusing. In America alcoholism is accepted as a disease, whereas in Europe generally, it is not seen as a medical problem, and therefore hardly any funds are made available to find a 'medical solution'.

The definition of alcoholism remains vague but overall we can say that alcoholism is a form of problem drinking and involves a physical dependence on alcoholic drinks.

But what about the people affected by it? Are they interested in a fancy definition? Probably not. Partners, family members and friends of alcoholics are trying to make sense of a life out of control, a life of lies. People are trying to make ends meet and there is desperation and often violence, both verbally and physically. They don't care about fancy studies and conclusions and are more interested in advice on living with an alcoholic and how to help an alcoholic.

The alcoholic, held hostage by the alcohol, feels alone and in deep conflict with those around him and deep down inside, also with him or herself. They probably know the problems alcohol abuse can cause. They probably know what it must mean to their loved ones to live with an alcoholic, but they feel there is no choice, that there is no way out. Only escape through the numbing effect of alcohol to cover possible feelings of guilt and the apparent easy solution of denial. Alcoholism and its definition are irrelevant and empty terms.

Alcoholism isn't even defined by the amount a person drinks, but by the effect drinking has on any area of someone's life, such as:

• Arguments with family and friends about how much someone should drink

• Lying or hiding your drinking habits

• Needing a drink so you can relax

- Not remembering what you did during a drinking session (black out)

- Rather spending money on alcohol than on food

- Drinking to feel better about yourself

- Drinking more than you intended to on a regular basis

- Drinking while you know it can be physically dangerous, like drinking and driving

- Neglecting your responsibilities at home and/or at work

- Using alcohol as a self-medication for other health problems, such as anxiety, depression, etc.

- Relying on alcohol to function

- Feel physically compelled to have a drink, for example shaking.

For someone who can recognise him or herself in one or more of the above-stated behaviours the definition of alcoholism is not so relevant. What is important is understanding and the realisation that alcoholism is about pain and frustration, about living a lie, about insecurity and overcoming obstacles, but above all, about human beings.

FACTS ABOUT ALCOHOL

Findings in case of alcoholics differ from person to person. Mostly, the level of consumption of alcohol determines certain features about an alcoholic. Basically alcoholism is a constant disorder, which is accompanied with habitual consumption of alcohol causing serious damage to person's health and mind. Even social and professional activities are deteriorated due to alcoholism habit.

Symptoms

Some familiar symptoms of alcoholism include continuous craving for alcohol, physical dependence on others, loss of memory, loss of appetite and numbness in body parts. This is an accepted fact about alcohol that if once you get into the grip of alcoholism, then in spite of strong urge to keep yourself away from it, it is difficult to do it. You always try to stop drinking but you do not find yourself capable of doing it and at the end you resort back to alcohol. Your alcohol tolerance level needed for extended amount of alcohol increases every time you go for drinking.

Factors Responsible for Alcohol Abuse

There are many factors responsible for alcoholism which includes social causes, environmental reasons and most importantly genetic causes. Generally, the disease of alcoholism is not dependent on the type of alcohol you are consuming, but the factors which affect it greatly include the duration of addiction, quantity of consumption of alcohol and excessive need to consume it. If the alcoholic is in first stage then it is easy to recover from but when it gets into final stage it is very hard to recover without sufficient medical prescription and supervision.

Myth about Alcohol

There are many health related facts about alcoholism. Excess consumption of alcohol leads to grave health problems. If you have recently taken to the alcohol you might suffer from problems like vomiting, loss of appetite, nausea, dizziness and gradually the loss of memory. If you continue it in long terms then you might have to undergo depression, liver cirrhosis, injury to liver, heart failure and failure of central nerve system.

You can easily understand the facts about alcoholism right from the initial warnings and symptoms. One known and popular fact about alcoholism is that it is a kind of drug addiction which can be physical and psychological. Facts about alcoholism are integrated with severe realities that alcoholism is a main cause for decreased activity level and energy amount in the body. It increases the sense of insecurity in alcoholic and affects his or her body system. It can even result in gastrointestinal tract irritation which might be accompanied with corrosion of the esophagus, fatigue, vomiting and stomach linings.

Many other facts about alcoholism are that alcoholism and caffeine are the most widely abused substance, according to a recent research. But on account of alcohol related accidents it is considered more severe problem. There are two ways of alcohol consumption; one is alcohol abuse and the other is alcohol dependence. Alcohol dependence is most harmful as its consequences are characterized by forbearance and withdrawal. Tolerance or forbearance means increased curiosity to drink more for extra intoxication. Withdrawal symptoms appear after discontinuing the regular intake of alcohol. Alcohol abusers are those alcoholics who often drink heavily and then get involved in problems like accidents and missing work.

There are a number of facts associated with alcohol which can drastically affect not only your social life but your work also. If you are aware about these facts then you can save yourself from many grave problems.

Chapter 2: I Am Addicted" Is A

Decision

Indeed, it turns out that a person ultimately makes a diagnosis of "dependence" on his own. This is no longer a diagnosis, but a decision made forever.

In our life, we make not so many such decisions. These are such decisions as: choosing a religion, choosing a bride (or groom), choosing a profession, choosing a place of residence. I am an alcoholic; this is the fifth decision from this series. Here, on the fingers of one hand and counted to five …

Such decisions can only be made by responsible people. That is why alcoholism is extremely interested in ensuring that its slaves never grow up. Often you have to see "teenagers" at 50, 60, and even 70 years old. In the conversation, they show some coquetry, look away, turn the conversation to another topic, or, conversely, gaining false courage, shut up, as if in interrogation, sternly looking to the side. Such a patient all the time wants to end the conversation with the famous phrase of a teenage bully: "I will not be scolded anymore!"

In fact, the person who made this decision has a certificate "I have matured to old age." Unfortunately, not everyone succeeded.

All of these have something in common:

Firstly, these are decisions that are made without logic, without evidence, without theorizing, without reasoning, without analyzing the past. Indeed, no one at the wedding asks the question: "What do you love for?" Such reasoning in such conditions seems tactless and meaningless.

In such cases, the answer "Yes" is yes, and the answer "No, maybe yes" is regarded as the answer "No." The main idea is that if evidence is needed, then there is doubt. You cannot prove to yourself: I am an alcoholic. Now you will prove it to yourself, and then just as convincingly prove yourself the opposite. This means that all intelligence will be aimed at refuting evidence when it will be beneficial for the disease. An alcoholic is a person who can pervert any logic. There is only one way out - there is no logic. No evidence is needed; there will be no rebuttal.

In no case should you stop drinking because "everything is bad." This is all bad now; then everything will not be so bad, and then completely good. Hundreds of times, I had to see people who sat down and said: "That's it! I lost my job, family, and health. I need to stop drinking!" It seems convincing; the person has arguments. But, a month or two passes, and he finds work, after six months it seems that his health has recovered, and there the family appeared. And then the most terrible begins - he begins to drink again.

You can't give up for the sake of the family, for the sake of children, for the sake of work - this is blackmail. Such decisions are made for their own sake without conditions. At the same time, if discussions about heredity and references to psychoanalysis begin, it means that there was no solution. This condition is unstable.

A conversation on this topic often begins with a description of the past. Sometimes the doctor becomes the initiator of these memories. You can understand the doctors - he wants to collect an anamnesis to assess the stage of the disease. But, unfortunately, many patients perceive such issues as an occasion to "confession." The "criminal during interrogation" behavior model begins to work: you need to admit to the little things in order to hide the main thing.

As a rule, a conversation starts "from afar":

- Five years ago, I received a doctor's order for 1 year and did not drink 1 year and two months...

So I want to "continue":

- So, maybe you are not an alcoholic since you received more than the doctor planned?

The decision is forever taken on the basis of the here and now principle. It does not matter, by and large, how the disease developed - slowly or quickly, paroxysmally or smoothly. What happened before the day you recognized yourself as a patient should no longer affect the direction of thought, as it may affect the recovery period.

Secondly, such decisions are made without taking into account the opinions of others. No one can know what to do in such a situation. In making such a decision, the person declares: "I do not know how to, I know how I need to." No matter how close the interlocutor is, authoritative, in such matters, everyone warrants for himself. There are no right or wrong in such decisions.

One has to see how, after talking with the doctor, the patient ends up in a company where some professor claims that sometimes it is necessary to drink. Say, alcohol washes away plaques on the vessels, relieves stress, and, in general, drunkenness is our national trait. Is it necessary to explain what decision the alcoholic will make after this conversation, whose arguments will seem more convincing to him. Do not even argue with such a professor. He speaks correctly. He needs to drink - well, let him drink. And if some prominent actor or minister will recommend me who to marry, which church to go to, whom to work with? Such "advice" can only be taken as a stupid joke. This does not mean that my interlocutor is stupid or a person whose opinion is not worth listening to. This is simply not his business. One train went left, the other right. Which of the drivers is wrong? Yes, no one, they go in different directions. No need to teach anyone to live. And let no one teach you this either. Each has its own fate, its own choice.

If an alcoholic begins to hate drunkards, he is annoyed by the advertisement of alcohol; he fights against alcoholism around the world - this means that the topic itself is not indifferent to him. He is still there in the affected area. This is a huge risk to him. After all, hatred is the sister of envy.

Thirdly, such decisions always force a change in lifestyle. It is important to understand that sobriety is not just dryness. This is a state of mind, a stage in a person's life. The stage, which not everyone reaches, just as not all were soldiers, students, not everyone marries. Absolutely everyone stops drinking, but the happy ones succeed in life.

It always happens, he remains the same as he was, nothing happens. If a person decided to become military personnel, then a lot will have to be changed. Remaining "in the soul" of civilian service, you will turn service into torture; you cannot resign as a general.

Also, in sobriety, preserving all the luggage and not acquiring new, a person remains the same deeply sick, easily vulnerable. One of my patients, realizing this, said: "I simulated sobriety for two years."

Many understand that it is necessary to change and make a typical mistake, starting to change their lifestyle. They declare: "I will be good. I'm giving up drinking, smoking; I'll be faithful to my wife and go in for sports!" It seems that everything is right, but nothing will come of it. Such a person will have to test willpower for strength, and, as we have said, the willpower of an alcoholic is not in his hands. It seems otherwise, but it is not always clear who controls a change to drinking habits.

You Need to Start by Changing Priorities

Initially, a person changes priorities, as determined by a goal. Then the way of thinking changes, and the way of life changes by itself. As in the example of the military: at the beginning, the man had a

24

goal - to become a general. He took the oath, learned the charter, serves. For this, the boots are not heavy, and the uniform is beautiful, and the service is not a burden. In a few years, it will not be clear to him why not everyone is in service. What seems difficult and incomprehensible to civilians will be easy and taken for granted. The lifestyle is like a large barge, which was built and loaded for more than one year, and even ten. Standing on the deck, it is very easy to turn such a ship. Everything is simpler - you need to move the anchor, and then it itself will turn with the current.

Willpower and courage will be needed only to make a decision: "I need Sobriety!" With this in mind, a person gradually begins to think differently, and then he does not recognize himself that he has changed so much.

It is very typical that, stepping into sobriety, filled with the desire to preserve it, at all costs, many are preparing themselves to be provoked. Whole phrases are prepared (sometimes with obscene language), which can be used to refuse drinking. It's funny, but it turns out that these "bombs" are not needed. The patients themselves say: "I suggested a couple of times, I refused, and no one insisted ..."In any case, when there is a goal, these problems go away by themselves. You just have to be firm. This is one of the first steps to treating your sick mind.

Chapter 3: What Is Overdose?

An overdose is a biological response your body gives when it receives a lot of substance or combination of chemicals. An overdose could be intentional or accidental. People can overdose on illegal drugs, alcohol, prescribed medications, and many other substances. Often, overdoses are fatal, however, a lot of people who have overdosed could be saved if treatment is provided immediately. Overdose happens to be the leading cause of many accidental deaths in America. In the case of drugs, there are various ways your body could become overwhelmed by substances. However, the most frequent cause of death of any chemical overdose is respiratory failure.

Depressant Overdose

Depressants that affect the central nervous system (CNS), include opioids, benzodiazepines, and alcohol consumption. Drugs that are CNS depressants lower blood pressure and body temperature; slows heartbeat and breathing. That's the reason these drugs cause sedative effects, which result in anxiety and an increase in calm and ecstatic effect. When an excessive amount of depressants is used, it could result in adverse effects, such as respiratory failure, overdose, coma, and even death

Opioid Overdose

Opioids are one of the natural drugs to overdose on, given how they react when taken. Your body provides opioid receptors in different areas, in the brain, central and peripheral nervous systems, as well as the gastrointestinal tract. When someone uses opioids, these receptors are activated and slow the body down. Whenever your body becomes overwhelmed by opioids, several receptors are blocked, and it can't perform other functions. This will result in a higher risk of overdosing, which can decelerate a person's breathing. Different opioids may be severe, where it could take minutes for a person who took heroin to experience the consequences from the overdose, someone who uses fentanyl will feel it within minutes. These powerful opioids are the reason the President of America declared a national opioid epidemic in 2017.

What is Naloxone?

Naloxone is an essential weapon in the fight against opioid overdose, Naloxone popularly made from Narcan, is an opioid antagonist that will stop the effects of opioids on the body. If someone takes an overdose, and the condition is severe, several doses of Narcan can stop the severity, and save the person's life. Narcan is available without prescription in America.

Alcohol Overdose

An alcohol overdose happens when you drink more alcohol than your body can safely process. Generally, the body can process around one unit of alcohol each hour (approximated to be the amount of alcohol in a shot of liquor, a half-pint of beer, or 1 glass of wine).

If a person drinks more alcohol than this within a short while, the alcohol accumulates in the body because the body cannot metabolize the alcohol fast enough, and a build-up of alcohol spreads throughout your body. This may result in alcohol overdose referred to as alcohol poisoning.

Symptoms of alcohol poisoning include:

Mental confusion.

Vomiting.

Seizures.

Slow breathing.

Irregular breathing.

Hypothermia, bluish epidermis, paleness

Factors that influence your risk of having an alcohol overdose include:

Age.

Gender.

Body Size.

Tolerance.

Binge Drinking

Drug Use

Other medical issues

Additional risks that can occur due to drinking more amounts of alcohol than the body can metabolize are:

Slower breathing, gag reflex, and decreased heartbeat.

Cardiac arrest attributed to a decrease in body temperature (hypothermia).

constant seizures attributed to low blood sugar

Stimulant Overdose.

Stimulants, such as meth or cocaine, concentrate on the CNS, however, on the other hand, opioids increase heartbeat, blood circulation pressure, body temperature, and breathe. A stimulant overdose occurs when the heart, the respiratory system, or blood circulation system is overworked to a point of wearing down.

Symptoms of stimulant overdose include:

Jerking or stiff limbs.

Rapid increase in body temperature or a sudden outburst of high fever.

Increasing pulse.

Loss of consciousness.

Seizures or convulsions.

Chest pain.

Severe headaches.

Excessive sweating.

Irritability and agitation.

Disorientation or mental confusion.

Severe hypertension.

Delirium.

Stroke.

Cardiac arrest.

Cardiovascular arrest.

Abnormal or shallow breathing

Some medications can help reduce or stabilize symptoms, such as blood pressure, pulse, body temperature, and any respiratory disorder. There are also medications you could use to help someone who experiences convulsions or seizures, such as anti-epileptic medications. Getting the person to the nearest hospital as soon as you can help save a life.

Getting Help for Overdose

Remember that treating overdose at home won't be the same as getting help from a hospital. Even if the patient seems to have recuperated, there is still a chance that a relapse might occur or that something is going on in the body the patient is not aware of. Taking the patient to a hospital will make a lot of difference in whether the patient will survive or die.

Overdose is a frightening term, it is often associated with death, however, it doesn't always lead to it. Life continues after treatment from an overdose, but the patient must understand the concept and learn from it.

Recovery isn't something that is accomplished quickly, however, it's possible, and not only that, there's also a guarantee that the patient might never suffer an overdose again.

If you don't know how to go about it, or you need help for someone you love, please speak to a treatment specialist. They're there, 24/7 to answer any questions you may have, whether it's for yourself or someone else.

Chapter 4: Support Groups (Friends And Family)

When you are attempting to kick your drinking habit for good, it is a great idea to have as much outside support as possible. You are most likely not going to be successful if you attempt to do it completely on your own with absolutely no help and/or support. Your close friends and family can offer you a lot of the support you are certainly going to need. You should make an honest effort and reach out to all of those close to you whom you feel you can trust to give you that support.

Those first few weeks after you initially stop drinking are most likely going to be the moat difficult. You want to identify your triggers and your friends and family can help you do this. They can usually help you see and understand reasons behind your drinking that you might not be able to realize and understand on your own.

You are going to want to try and figure out what the underlying reasons are that make you want to drink in the first place. Some people drink when they feel stressed out and/or anxious. They want to pick up an alcoholic beverage because it helps to "calm their nerves" and helps them relax. If stress and/or anxiety is a major cause for your drinking problem, you can implement a new habit. Whenever you began to feel stressed and/or anxious, instead of picking up an alcoholic beverage, pick up the phone and call a close friend or family member. They can help you talk about whatever it is that is making you feel stressed out and /or causing your anxiety. Chances are, just being able to talk about things with someone close to you can help you calm down and ease a lot of your anxiety symptoms. It an also help take your mind of wanting to drink. This is one example of how your friends and family can help support you in your efforts to stop drinking for good.

Another way your support circle can help you stay sober is by helping to keep you occupied so that your desire to drink alcohol becomes less and less of an issue for you. Being able to call someone for help whenever you are struggling with your desire to drink is a great thing, and having someone who can come over and take you out somewhere is an ever better thing. Your family and friends can offer social support for you as well. They can help you find better, more suitable places to hang out and socialize where there is no alcohol available.

When you were drinking, you probably hung out in bars and other places where alcohol was regularly served. If you seriously want to be able to stay sober, you are going to need to find other places to hang out in. You can have a close friend or family member accompany you to a sober hang out spot, like a coffee shop or a diner where no alcohol is served.

Chapter 5: Initiating Concrete Measures To Ward Off Your Alcohol Consumption Tendencies

The most crucial step in overcoming alcohol addiction lies in being honest to yourself. As stated in the previous chapter, one of the symptoms of alcohol addiction is the refusal to admit that there's a problem. This denial serves not only as a defense mechanism for the alcoholic, but is also a potent way to justify one's continued intake of alcoholic drinks.

As such, if you are indeed sincere about your desire to live an alcohol-free life, at the very least you must be brave and honest enough to admit that you have a problem and that you need help. Doing so can allow you to take stock of your situation and raise your sense of responsibility and accountability for your overall sense of well-being. This admission can then be your precursor to initiate concrete measures to rid yourself of your alcohol addiction. If you have purchased this book then you have likely already come to this conclusion, which is a great step forward.

The actions below can be followed as the initial steps to treating your alcohol addiction.

1. Accept Your Addiction

As mentioned above, unless you accept and acknowledge that you do in fact have an addiction to alcohol that you want to be free from, you will continue in a state of denial and will not be able to address your alcoholism.

2. Set Goals

As with all aspects of life, a key ingredient to success is goal-setting for yourself. Without goal-setting it becomes easy to forget what you are trying to achieve and to fall back into old habits. Your goals could include the more obvious, like being completely sober, but can also include the positive effects of your sobriety, including better finances and stronger relationships, for example. It's important to paint a positive picture of the life you will lead once you free yourself of your alcohol addiction. Doing so will give you something to strive for, particularly on days where overcoming the addiction is more difficult for you. It is also important to write down your goals and even to say them out-loud, both to yourself and to those you trust. This will help to reinforce your goals and keep you accountable.

3. See Your Doctor and Make A Plan

After reading this book, you should take the time to turn the recommendations into a plan that has dates. Your plan should include the answers to questions like, "How long will it take before I can be completely alcohol-free?", and "What will I do if fall into a relapse"? Writing down this plan will also help to reinforce your goals and break down those goals into more manageable steps.

Before making this plan, it is important to seek the guidance of your doctor. Your doctor should have a number of treatment options that can be provided to you and they will likely know of resources in your community that you can tap into for support. While you should follow your doctor's guidance, a number of prevalent treatment options have been noted below.

4. Treat Your Addiction

A) Detoxify By Going "Cold Turkey"

Going "cold turkey" means completely ridding yourself of your addiction right away. In the case of alcohol it would mean stopping the consumption of all alcoholic beverages in one go. Going cold turkey is advisable for those whose addiction condition has not reached extreme or alarming levels just yet. The first order of the day should be to throw all your alcohol away. Do a complete search of your home, including the nooks and crevices where you usually hide alcohol. Once done, pour everything down the drain. Due emphasis should be placed on the word "everything." Be uncompromising when it comes to discarding all of your alcohol.

If you have expensive wines or liquors and you can't bear to throw good money down the sink, then you can always give them to other people. But make sure the people you give them to are people whom you trust and believe to have no alcohol problem themselves.

B) Detoxify Gradually

If you believe that going cold turkey would be too extreme a route for your alcohol addiction, you could attempt to gradually lower your intake on a week-by-week basis. If you go this route though, you must plan carefully how much alcohol that you will consume each week and you must hold yourself accountable to these limits. This is risky because many people will feel tempted to drink more alcohol after the first drink, and it is only recommended for those who have good support systems in place that can help to keep them accountable. This could include family or friends. Regardless of whether detoxification is by the cold turkey method or by a more gradual reduction, your doctor should be consulted to help select the best method for you.

C) Medications

There are several drugs that have been approved in the United States that may help to reduce your desire for alcohol, or that purposely give you unpleasant symptoms when you consume alcohol. These drugs should be non-addictive and may assist some people in overcoming their alcohol addiction and/or maintaining their sobriety. While medications may help control the urge to drink, they will not resolve the underlying reasons for your addiction, and should therefore be combined with other forms of treatment. Speak with your doctor to learn more about these medications. For non-US individuals, you can still speak with your doctor to see what medications may be available in your country.

D) Addictions Support Groups

There are a number of support groups available that assist people to overcome their alcohol addiction. These group may have their own methodology for helping you to successfully become sober. One of the more popular groups is Alcoholics Anonymous, which uses a 12-step program to help achieve sobriety. In this set-up, you are basically provided the space to talk about your feelings, your experiences, the things that drove you to resort to alcohol, and the steps you are currently taking to claim your life back from your addiction.

You also get to listen to other people who know exactly what you are going through because they have been or are going through the same thing. This is a great way to learn about what has worked or not worked for others.

These groups can both aid your treatment by providing a set treatment program, and by providing you with the support of other people who are going through the same journey that you are in trying to become sober.

E) Identifying and Addressing Your Triggers

As mentioned in a previous chapter, there are likely certain things in your life that trigger your desire for a drink. This could include work or family stress, or some feeling of insecurity, or it could be related to more fun activities like watching sports or spending time with friends. Whatever the cause, it's important that you understand what your triggers are. The next step is to either avoid these triggers (which may not always be possible) or to develop means of addressing them that don't involve alcohol. Ideally, you should respond to your triggers in a healthy way, like physical activity, or talking with friends, family or a counselor. To reiterate, it is extremely important to identify and understand what your triggers are, otherwise it will be easy to fall back into old habits and keep drinking.

F) Counseling

Counseling can be a means of addressing both the root causes of your alcohol addiction and the triggers in your life that draw you towards alcohol. Some counselors may help you to come to terms with underlying aspects of your life that could be driving you to alcohol, such as family history or anxiety or depression, for example. Behavioral counseling on the other hand, can help you to identify how you respond to triggers in a given moment with the aim of adjusting your behavior so that you no longer drink once you've been triggered. An example of a trigger could simply be when you are with friends and one of them offers you a drink; behavioral therapy could help you to think differently in this situation and reject the drink rather than accepting it out of habit.

G) Spiritual Practice

While not everyone is spiritual or religious, many people find solace in spirituality and a spiritual or religious community. Many spiritual and religious organizations do not condone alcoholism, and may have their own treatment programs and support groups in place to help individuals within their community to deal with their addiction. Counseling may also be offered by religious or spiritual leaders within these communities. If you are part of a spiritual or religious organization, it may be worth investigating what support programs you have access to.

Chapter 6: The Game Plan

If you are reading this book, it means that you want to quit and that's good news but you should be mentally prepared. Quitting is hard and this truth should not be sugar-coated. On the bright side, new developments in medical science, psychological counseling, integrated communities and spiritual meditation makes it easier to quit.

Before you take a step on your own, talk to a doctor or to somebody who has been through this. Don't stop drinking abruptly because you will feel withdrawal symptoms that may prove to be very dangerous for you, even life-threatening in severe cases. Your body and mind depends on it and you need to do it in steps. Set a concrete goal that you can achieve. Give yourself time, analyze your strengths and weaknesses, and see how you can do it. Don't let guilt get in the way because it will only make the matters worse and it might take you back to this habit. Accept that you did something harmful but now that you have decided to quit, you will set things right.

Talk to a Doctor

You simply don't have to do it alone. It is always better to talk to a doctor and get his advice. Medical practitioners will help you better than anyone else because they are experts and they treat everyone according to their condition. They usually help to minimize withdrawal symptoms through medicines like Benzodiazepines. These are psychoactive drugs that help to calm anxiety and control panic attacks.

After you have talked to your doctor or a psycho-therapist, it is time to sit down and think about your strategy that will not only help you now but also in the long-run.

Your doctor will not be at your home; he will simply give you a general layout of what to do and what 'not' to do and prescribe medicines. The rest lies entirely upon you. If you have a serious problem of alcohol addiction that cannot be treated at home, then it's better to go to a rehabilitation centre. If not, you should make a plan that will work for you.

Set Achievable Goals

Goal setting is the most important part of making positive changes in your life. Your goals will make everything systematic and it will be easier to keep track of this important phase of your life, when you are trying to quit. It will also give you a sense of purpose which will help you to deal with your stress and heighten your spirits. Don't set general aims, break them down to categories and put the "stop drinking alcohol" goal under the health category.

Be honest with yourself because you know yourself better than anyone. You know your strengths and weaknesses, so you should set goals that you can achieve. Set a timeline that is suitable for you and write down the date somewhere or mark it on the calendar for a better understanding of what you are doing. This date can be set for a few weeks, a few months or a year's time. After setting the date, it is important to acknowledge what you can do and what you cannot do. Do not be hard on yourself. If you cannot do it fast, you don't have to. You can simply start by discarding the recipes which require alcohol. While setting your goals, it is time to look deep down into your inner self. You will then understand the significance of "know thyself". It's not simply about knowing yourself; it is also about accepting who you are and what you can do to improve yourself. Guilt can increase your need to drink, so it's better to embrace yourself and your family to achieve what seems to be very difficult to achieve now. Keeping these things in mind it will make your transition a whole lot easier.

Motivation Matters a Lot

When you are thinking about leaving alcohol, you need some kind of motivation. You should not simply do it for others or because someone wants you to change, you should do it for yourself. Having belief in yourself is very important to help you change. You should think about your past achievements, even the little ones matter. Recall how you achieved things like: how you passed an important exam, how you wrote a story, how you helped someone, how you made an important speech and what resources you used? If you achieved your goals before, you can do it now. Start by making a list of your talents and strengths that helped you to do things that matter to you. These positive thoughts will bring you out of that gloomy mood and give you a new energy.

After that, just imagine yourself achieving your goal "to stop drinking alcohol". Think of yourself engaged in other non-drinking activities like reading a book, going to a picnic, spending time with your family, gardening, learning to paint or decorating your home, and giving new spirits to your talents. If you imagine them, you can draw on these beautiful mind pictures and turn them into reality.

Now the final step towards this mental preparation is to think about this change as something positive. Change your attitude towards quitting. Your good side wants you to quit but your selfish half wants you to keep on drinking. Develop your will-power to such an extent that you can overcome your selfish half. Look around to some successful examples. Many people coped with a drinking problem or even smoking. If they can do it, then so can you. Change is a difficult process, so it's better to break it down into smaller steps. These steps will be explained in the next chapter.

Keep a Diary

If you don't write in a diary, it's time for you to keep one and also write in it. It should be more like a "drinking diary". You should record your activities, like when you drink, record the when, why, where and with who did you drink. Also, mention the time when you had no cravings and you drank less. You should also write when you drink a lot and you were experiencing cravings more than usual. When you write, mention the date on the top of the page. These diary entries will help you to better understand your situation, avoid the situations where you will most likely drink, and focus on the activities that help you to control your cravings.

Write about your feelings as well. Write every day and mention how your day went, were you feeling depressed or you were ill. If you had a hangover, pour your feelings on the paper, even if you feel really bad. This will help you to make a decision to not drink so heavily. Then double check on your list of the situations where you yearned to drink.

While writing in the diary, you can tell your story to yourself. Imagine that you are listening to a friend who is telling you about his/her problems. If you become the "other person", you can see your situation from a different perspective. Imagine what advice you would give to that friend of yours. Who knows what you will discover from this practice, a talent to observe, listen, imagine and tell a story. You will almost become an artist who conveys everything by writing. It will be an amazing experience.

Family Support

If you are losing your relationships, it's time to tell them about your intentions, tell them how important they are to you, apologize to them and take them to your doctor. When they talk to your doctor, they will believe you. You have got to work to rebuild that bridge of trust between you and your family. If they are very angry, fight with you or even thinking about leaving you, you should not quarrel back. It's hard to overlook the painful comments and arguments but it will work. If they say that you are never there for them and you only think about yourself, change this statement to a question. The other person will have to elaborate this statement and this will give you a chance to listen to their feelings and tell them about yours. If you cannot make up with them, you should not lose hope. You should accept that and keep on with your efforts to change. If your family agrees to live with you or better yet, forgive you; capitalize on it as your biggest strength. When they support you, it will give you a new strength and this change will be easier than ever because you will not be alone in your efforts!

Think about the Money you spent on Alcohol

Try to estimate how much you spend on alcohol every week. Multiply this number with the number of weeks, months or years you have been drinking and look at this huge number! Then think about what you could do with that money if you didn't buy alcohol. For instance, you could give it in charity, go on a vacation, spend it on your home's maintenance, invest it in a business or secure your children's future. You can do lots of things with the money you save by not buying alcohol. Keep these possibilities in your goal "to stop drinking alcohol".

After thinking about all these aspects and taking these steps, you can jump to the next stage, the real one, where you will learn how to practically implement your thoughts into your life. These steps will help you to prepare yourself for the more important tasks ahead and to cleanse your body and mind from this poison.

Chapter 7: Steps To The Path Of Recovery

Your journey to recovery from alcohol dependency can start today. If you are committed to making a change in your life, you can do it. Do not wait until you hit rock bottom to take action. As bumpy as the road may get and as long as the journey may be, you can overcome alcohol addiction. All you need is the willingness to admit that you have a problem, and get the necessary medical and social support. In this chapter, you will learn about seven steps that you can take for alcohol treatment and recovery.

Step 1: Make a Commitment to Stop Drinking Alcohol

The majority of people who suffer from alcohol addiction tend to approach the recovery process gradually. It is difficult to find someone with an alcohol problem deciding to stop drinking overnight. Denial is usually a huge challenge for alcoholics, especially during the early stages of the change process. You may find yourself making excuses as to why you are not ready to do it, or start dragging your feet when it comes to taking concrete action to stop drinking. Admitting your problem is never enough. You have to be willing to take the necessary action. One of the most effective ways to deal with being indecisive about quitting is to compare the costs and benefits of your decision.

You should consider making a table to compare the benefits of drinking to the benefits of not drinking. You should also make another table comparing the costs of drinking to the costs of not drinking. For example:

Benefits of drinking:

•It helps me unwind and release stress after work

•It helps me have fun and enjoy myself

•I don't have to think about my problems for a little while

Benefits of not drinking:

•I get to spend more time with my family and have more energy for my hobbies

•It would probably improve the state of most of my relationships

•I would feel better physically and mentally

Costs of drinking:

•It takes away the time and energy for my family or to improve my performance at work

•It brings problems in my relationships

•It makes me feel embarrassed, anxious, and depressed.

Costs of not drinking:

•My drinking buddies won't like me anymore

•I would be forced to face the responsibilities I have abandoned

•I would be forced to find another outlet for my problems

Step 2: Set and Commit To Your Goals

Establish specific, measurable, attainable, realistic, and time-conscious goals. If you want to, you can set a specific date on which you will stop drinking. Alternatively, you can set a goal to stop drinking on weekdays as from a certain date. You could also set a goal to limit the number of drinks you have on week-days. You can choose to have a few drinks on the weekends. Your goal could be to stop completely or cut back, but you have to set a definitive date.

Once you have set your goals, you should note down some of the ways you plan on achieving these goals. These can include:

•Remove all temptations of alcohol from your home or office

•Tell everyone your goal so that they can support you and hold you accountable

•Set limits in your life. Tell your family that no alcohol is allowed in the home and inform friends that you cannot attend events where alcohol is served.

•Kick your alcoholic friends to the curb. Painful as this may be, you do not want to hang around people who don't support your decision to quit.

•Maintain a 'drinking diary' and note down every time you drink alcohol. Track your alcohol consumption for about a month and then see how you can reduce it further.

•Sip your drink slowly. Take a break between drinks and have some food, juice, or water. Don't forget to eat when you are out drinking.

Step 3: Safety First

If you can handle the effects of alcohol withdrawal on your own, then do it. There are people who need to be hospitalized in order to undergo safe withdrawal. The option you choose will depend on the duration of your addiction, the quantities you've been consuming, and how healthy your body is.

Step 4: Build a New Life

Even though professional treatment is a great first step, you need to stay away from alcohol for the long term. This means that you have to hit the reset button and find new meaning for your life. You can achieve this by:

•Finding a strong support group. Find a group of recovering addicts, or surround yourself with people who love you and will encourage your positive life choices. Invest in the community around you because this will help you stay motivated to make the right choices.

•Taking better care of yourself. Embark on an exercise program, eat healthy food and get enough sleep. This will help you avoid cravings, release stress, and boost your emotional health.

•Finding new interests and hobbies. You can volunteer your time or find work that makes you feel fulfilled. As long as you feel good about yourself you will not think about your old lifestyle.

Step 5: Prepare For Cravings and Drinking Triggers

The first six months are the hardest when it comes to dealing with alcohol cravings and potential triggers. You can control your cravings using the following techniques:

•Find an activity to distract you until the craving passes. You can go for a run, listen to some music, or engage in some housekeeping. Anything that helps you take your mind off of your craving is a good idea.

•Find somebody you trust and talk to them. The moment the urge comes upon you, pick up the phone or go to your sponsor, a friend or relative who supports you, or a member of your faith community. They will help you stay focused and accountable to your alcohol recovery program.

•Think about the negative effects alcohol has had on your life. When a craving strikes, your mind has the tendency to think back to the good effects that alcohol had on you. Replace those thoughts with reasons why drinking won't make your life better.

•Be patient and wait for the urge to dissipate. Rather than fight the craving, just let it ride over you like a wave. Once it peaks, it will start dissipating and soon disappear.

Step 6: Find Support

You will definitely need moral support, guidance, comfort, and encouragement if you are to succeed in your recovery. It doesn't matter what kind of treatment you are undergoing – self-help, rehab, or medical therapy – support makes a huge difference. There are a number of ways that you can get support:

•Join an alcoholic recovery support group and make sure that you attend their meetings. Such groups are very helpful because you get to interact with other people who understand your struggles and can share their stories with you. They will teach you how to stay sober and get you through the tough times.

•Get support from family and friends. If you are afraid to turn to your relatives because of the shame or guilt brought on by past behavior, consider attending family therapy. This will help the entire family sort through any issues related to your alcoholism.

•Build a new social network. Since you have left your old life and friends behind, you need to make new connections. You could join a church group or class, volunteer, or attend community events.

•Move to a sober living home. In case your home does not offer a supportive environment to stay sober, you could consider moving into a sober living home. They provide support and a safe environment for recovering addicts.

Step 7: Start Your Treatment

Addiction takes a huge toll on the body as well as the mind. Therefore, you should consider seeing a mental health professional and look into some advanced addiction programs. Alcohol abuse tends to be accompanied by depression, bipolar disorder, and anxiety, so it's important to get treatment for your psychological issues as well.

What you need to remember is that alcoholism treatment does not have a magic bullet. There are some treatments that will work for some people but not others. This is why you need to find a program that will be customized to fit you. The treatment you receive should take into account your entire lifestyle, including your relationships, health, and career. Finally, you need to remain committed to your recovery program. Follow through on your treatment no matter how long it takes.

Chapter 8: Change The Way You Live

After the person has changed the way he or she thinks, it is time to change the way he or she lives. This is the time when what they have thought of, they do it with conviction. They do not just create a mission or an objective but that they do something about the objective that they have created. Thus, at this point, it is time to create a plan, which the person does, to make sure that they would be able to fulfill their objective, which is to stop alcohol addiction and abuse. At this stage, they create strategies that would lead them to overcoming their alcohol addiction.

For instance, it would be good to create alternative coping skills, as they face this difficulty of trying to give up the habit of taking more alcohol than what is really necessary. These coping skills can be done by making sure that bad habits are being replaced by good ones. As it has been said, bad habits are not broken but are being replaced with new ones. Thus, these alternative skills may include the initiative of trying to recognize their rewards for trying to quit drinking. Rewards are really useful, especially when people face tasks that are quite difficult to achieve over a period of time.

They should think of what they will soon get once they have succeeded in lessening their intake of alcohol, once they develop the ability of being able to control their cravings. Experts have mentioned the necessity of having positive thoughts when trying to fulfill tasks. They said that these positive thoughts can calm the minds of people, and it can take away the anxiety and the worry of not knowing how to start or end the task. It can lift the spirit and give an inspiring message both to the mind and the spirit, that the pain may be removed in replacement of something that is more worthwhile to think of and to possess. As it is once said, one cannot just take something away without putting something in replacement of it. There has to be something to fill up the emptiness and the vacancy, for in this the coping mechanisms begins to work out, and the person will not be going back to where he or she has been before the dilemma began taking place.

Secondly, it is important to make lifestyle changes. These would start in the little things that the person does, such as cleaning their cupboards of all the alcoholic beverages that once were aligned in a variety. They can also try to prevent going to parties or drinking sessions, wherein they tend to drink alcohol with their friends and associates. They may also try not to go to the clubs, or even theirfriends'house, where they tend to drink alcohol without limit. Likewise, they may try to drink black coffee instead, whenever they feel like trying to drink another bottle of alcohol. Others would rather smoke some cigarettes, just to take away the cravings. All these may be little things, but they all mean a lot, especially when it comes to doing something that is really difficult to do or to achieve. Trying to overcome alcohol addiction is really difficult to achieve, which may be the reason why others would rather try and stop doing it with another friend or family member. Others do not do it alone. Instead, they find another person who is close to them, and they do their mission with this person and share with them their difficulties and what they have achieved so far. If another person is doing fine in his or her mission of trying to overcome alcohol addiction, the other one may become more motivated to give up drinking alcohol, since another person is doing the same task, meaning they are not alone in their ordeal. They have another person to express their difficulties with and what they have experienced so far, and that alone can give them the strength to overcome something that is difficult to give up, such as alcohol abuse and addiction.

Meanwhile, it would be best to use rewards once the person has succeeded in his or her mission over some period of time. If, for example, they have succeeded in trying to abstain from drinking alcohol, say for two months, then they should give themselves some rewards for being able to do that, such as giving themselves a treat or going to the movie and celebrating the day, since they have succeeded in their mission. They should acknowledge that they have indeed succeeded in their first stage, and the second stage would be to continue it for another two months, for example. By giving themselves some rewards, they finally acknowledge that they are indeed, making progress, and they have to motivate themselves a little bit more to make sure they continue with their mission for the upcoming months. However, they should never think of their mission as something to be done in too lengthy a time. Instead, they should think of their mission in stages or in smaller periods of time, such as every six months. They should never think of their mission as one that corresponds to eternity, and never think that there will be no other way of drinking alcohol or that never again would they be able to taste it. They should just do it one step at a time...and things will happen as planned.

Chapter 9: Negative Effects Of

Alcohol

The effect of alcohol sets in the moment you have the first sip. An occasional beer or a glass of wine with dinner doesn't cause any trouble, but when left unchecked, it can spell trouble. In mathematics, regardless of how complicated an equation might be, it must always be balanced, and the same principle is applicable in chemistry too. Any imbalance in the equation defeats its existence. Likewise, when the consumption of alcohol is left unchecked, it leads to alcohol use disorder. Everyone knows that consumption of alcohol is injurious to health. There are various statutory warnings stating the same on alcohol bottles. Why are these warnings in place? It is to warn the user of the negative consequences of drinking alcohol. So, what are these negative effects? In this section, let us look at how alcohol harms your overall health and wellbeing.

Central Nervous System

Alcohol has a deteriorative effect on the functioning of the central nervous system. The adverse effects include slurring of speech and coughing. Also, the consumption of alcohol harms the communication between the brain and the body. It is one of the leading reasons why people often lose consciousness after an episode of excessive drinking. Apart from it, you might also experience numbness or tingling sensation in your feet and arms. But the effect of alcohol on the central nervous system doesn't end here. It also harms your memory and makes it difficult for the brain to retain critical information. The frontal lobe of the brain is responsible for your short-term memory, regulation of emotions, and the skills required to make crucial decisions. It is the primary area of the brain that is negatively influenced by excessive alcohol intake. Therefore, it results in short-term memory loss, an inability to regulate emotions, and leads to poor decisions.

Inflammation

Your body has an inbuilt detoxifying system, and the liver is the primary organ that helps detoxify your body from within. The liver purifies all the toxic substances you consume, and anything harmful present within it is expelled from the body. However, your body is not a tireless machine, and all the organs present in it also require some rest. If they don't get the rest they deserve, then they don't function optimally. If you keep drinking, your liver must keep working on getting rid of the toxic buildup. Therefore, excessive and frequent consumption of alcohol harms your liver's ability to function.

If you keep drinking alcohol, believing that it does your body no harm, then the only person you are fooling is yourself. It is believed that the risk of chronic liver cancer and other liver diseases is quite high in all those who consume alcohol. Whenever you consume alcohol, some scar tissue is formed on the liver. As your alcohol intake increases, it results in the formation of excessive scar tissue. Once the liver is damaged, it becomes difficult for your body to remove toxic substances present within. So, in a way, the consumption of alcohol is leading to the buildup of toxic substances.

The scarring of the liver caused because of inflammation is known as cirrhosis. When left untreated, liver diseases can be life-threatening. Evidence suggests that the risk of liver diseases due to alcohol consumption is quite high in women when compared to men. It is believed that a woman's body requires longer to process and absorb all the alcohol they consume. Therefore, it results in slowing down the liver and triggers liver damage.

Sugar Levels

Whenever you consume any food, it is broken down into absorbable sugars by your body using a hormone known as insulin. The pancreas produces insulin, and it helps regulate the presence of glucose in the bloodstream. In all those who consume excessive alcohol and do so frequently, the chances of damage to the pancreas are quite high. When the pancreas and liver don't function optimally, it hinders the regular flow of sugar in the bloodstream. Whenever you consume any sugar, your pancreas manages it. With binge drinking, you are effectively preventing the pancreas from producing the required insulin for regulating sugar levels. When left unchecked, it leads to hyperglycemia. In hyperglycemia, the level of blood sugar is higher than what is required. Hyperglycemia is also known as diabetes. Diabetes is one of the risk factors of various other cardiovascular diseases and health conditions.

Digestive System

The relationship between alcohol consumption and the digestive system is not yet fully clear. However, once the digestive system is negatively affected because of alcohol consumption, the signs start slowly appearing. The more alcohol you drink and the longer you drink it, the higher will be the damage in your body. Excessive drinking results in intestinal damage and makes it incredibly difficult for your body to absorb and digest food optimally. If your body doesn't do either of these functions properly, it doesn't get the required nutrients. Over time, it can lead to various digestive troubles, such as bloating, diarrhea, and buildup of digestive gasses. Another common symptom of digestive difficulty caused due to excessive drinking is ulcers and trouble passing stools.

Once your digestive system doesn't function like it is supposed to, it becomes incredibly difficult for the body to absorb all the nutrients it requires. Excessive consumption of alcohol causes irreparable damage to cells present in the lining of the intestine and the stomach. It essentially blocks the absorption and the breakdown of important nutrients present in the food you consume. It also interferes with your body's ability to metabolize the nutrients it digests. It can also lead to an unhealthy suppression of appetite. When all these factors are put together, it leads to malnourishment.

Dependency

Addiction to alcohol is an illness. Regardless of what people might choose to believe, it is one of the steadily growing illnesses that have managed to severely affect the lives of millions across the world. Every year, millions fall prey to this disease, and it often proves fatal. Alcohol dependency is a condition wherein your body starts physically craving for and depending on alcohol to function normally. Alcohol dependency is also the first clue about alcohol addiction. Dependency also leads to alcohol withdrawal. Alcohol withdrawal is characterized by a state wherein an individual starts experiencing common withdrawal symptoms due to the absence of alcohol. As with any other addiction, dealing with withdrawal is essential for recovery. Plenty of people with alcohol dependency never seek the treatment they require because they are worried about facing the unpleasant effects of withdrawal. From chronic fatigue, irritability, and mood swings to nausea, cramps, and headaches, these are all symptoms of alcohol withdrawal.

Sexual Health

Consumption of alcohol reduces your inhibitions. It might make you feel more confident than you usually do. People also consume alcohol because they believe it gives them the best of confidence that they require to express themselves the way they want to, without any worries. Therefore, unsurprisingly, people drink alcohol believing that they will have more fun under the sheets. However, the real situation is contrary to these misinformed beliefs. One of the most common side effects of alcohol in men is erectile dysfunction. Also, women who drink excessively and frequently might suffer from rather painful and complicated pregnancies. Also, consumption of alcohol tends to have a severe effect on the health of the fetus in a pregnant woman. It is one of the reasons why women are advised to abstain from consuming alcohol during their pregnancy. The fetus's body directly absorbs anything that a mother consumes. So, alcohol will also be absorbed by the fetus. This can severely affect the growth of the fetus and might also lead to complications during birth. Alcoholism can run in the genes. So, the chances of the biological child of an alcoholic mother leaning toward alcoholism are quite high.

The Digestive and Endocrine System

The pancreas is responsible for triggering the release of digestive enzymes that enable your body to optimally digest and absorb the food you consume. Unfortunately, excessive intake of alcohol increases the regular production of these digestive enzymes and leads to a buildup. An excessive buildup of all these digestive enzymes is quite toxic for the body, and it results in a condition known as pancreatitis. Pancreatitis is also a risk factor for various other chronic illnesses and health complications. So, the next time you're tempted to consume another drink, just think about all the damage you are inflicting on your body.

Circulatory System

Consumption of alcohol also harms the health of your heart and lungs. Your heart needs to function optimally so that it keeps pumping blood to the rest of your body. When you start consuming alcohol, your heartbeat becomes abnormal. Excessive consumption of alcohol increases the risk of various cardiovascular diseases. It is also believed that women are at a greater risk of developing such diseases caused due to alcohol intake than men. Apart from an abnormal heartbeat, various other circulatory complications can crop up, such as high blood pressure, heart failure, heart diseases, strokes, or difficulties with the heart while pumping blood.

Immunity

Your immune system is your body's first line of defense against any possible illnesses. If the immune system is not strong enough, then any possible disease that comes your way will affect you. Excessive and prolonged consumption of alcohol weakens your immune system. Once your immune system is weakened, your body is left defenseless against potential illnesses. Two of the most rapidly growing diseases across the globe are pneumonia and tuberculosis. Excessive consumption of alcohol makes you likely to suffer from these issues. It is also believed that a significant percentage of tuberculosis cases are caused due to alcohol use disorder. There are a variety of other cancers that alcohol can result in, such as cancer of the breast, mouth, or colon.

Muscle and Skeletal Systems

Your musculature and skeletal structure are the core components on which your entire body lies. If you want to lead a happy and healthy life, then you need to have strong bones. Regardless of what it is, anything that you drink apart from water affects your body. These effects can be both good and bad. So, unsurprisingly, long-term consumption of alcohol is almost bad for your overall wellbeing. One of the long-term effects of alcohol consumption includes the weakening of bones. The risk of fracture and bone thinning is quite high in individuals who are frequently involved in binge drinking. Also, frequent and excessive consumption of alcohol can cause weakness in the muscles. It can lead to cramping, and when left unchecked, it can lead to muscle atrophy.

Physical Appearance

The consumption of alcohol not only deteriorates your internal health, but it also has other visible side effects. Frequent drinking leads to obesity. The term "beer belly" is used to refer to those individuals who have a pot belly primarily caused due to the consumption of a specific type of alcohol. In a way, excessive and regular consumption of alcohol deteriorates your physical appearance. Alcohol and obesity are directly related because excessive consumption of alcohol reduces your body's ability to burn fats effectively. When it doesn't burn fats, and instead, starts accumulating them, it leads to weight gain. Alcohol use disorder also dilates the blood vessels, and it gives the skin a ruddy and aged appearance. Therefore, it leads to premature aging of the skin.

Overall Behavior

Confusion, motor impairment, memory problems, and slurred speech are some of the immediate consequences of alcohol consumption. Therefore, frequent drinkers are at a greater risk of injuring themselves, getting involved in accidents, or engaging in violent behavior. Alcohol is a primary factor responsible for drowning, fatal burn injuries, and homicides too. It also plays a major role in most of the fatal motor vehicle accidents. Heavy drinking might prompt an individual to engage in risky sexual behavior, such as unprotected sex or even unintended sex. All these can lead to an increase in the risk of unintended pregnancies and sexually transmitted diseases.

The Brain

Alcohol use disorder or even alcohol abuse tends to cause certain long-term changes in your brain's chemistry. When you start drinking heavily for prolonged periods, the brain starts to counteract the slowing effects of alcohol by triggering the release of excitatory neurotransmitters. It does this so it can function optimally. Alcohol might make you feel happy for a while, but it essentially slows down your body. Since your body starts slowing down, your brain tries to counteract this by producing neurotransmitters that lead to more excitement.

Now, when your brain is in an excitable state, you require rather large doses of alcohol to achieve the results you previously desired. It, in turn, leads to a condition known as tolerance. You might also experience the rather unpleasant symptoms of withdrawal when you stop drinking suddenly. When all these changes are put together, it leads to an urge to drink, which ends up causing alcohol addiction and dependence.

Other types of brain damage can be caused due to frequent and excessive drinking, as the damage to the cerebellum. The cerebellum is the area of your brain responsible for coordination and balance. So, when this is affected, it becomes quite difficult to maintain overall balance and coordination. It can also cause involuntary tremors and involuntary back and forth eye movements (nystagmus). It can also lead to the development of peripheral neuropathy wherein the peripheral nervous system is damaged, which leads to weakening of muscles, tingling and burning pain in the extremities, and an overall sense of numbness. This sort of damage doesn't start immediately but takes a while to develop.

It is also believed that chronic drinking can lead to shrinkage in the cerebellum. The toxic effect of alcohol and its harmful effect on all the important nutrients the brain requires are the leading reasons for shrinkage in the cerebellum. This kind of damage can also harm the lower part of the brain known as the hypothalamus and the thalamus. When left unchecked, it leads to a fatal condition known as Wernicke-Korsakoff's syndrome. In this condition, it leads to loss of muscle coordination, memory loss, visual changes, and an inability to form any new memories whatsoever.

Psychological Effect

Drinking heavily and regularly might lead to the development of certain depression-related symptoms. Once again, it is all because the consumption of alcohol alters your brain chemistry. The levels of serotonin, a feel-good hormone that essentially regulates your mood, start reducing when you start drinking regularly. For some, anxiety or depression might have been the primary reason why they started drinking. That being said, it could be the other way around too. People might have started drinking, and then it could be the reason why they started experiencing anxiety or depression.

When you start drinking heavily, it tends to harm all the relationships in your life, regardless of whether it is your professional or personal relationships.

When your life doesn't seem to be going the way you wanted it to, it can lead to depression. Also, if you start using alcohol to mask your mood, or feel better, you are merely worsening the dependency on alcohol. All in all, it is a vicious cycle in which you keep going from consuming alcohol to feeling depressed, consuming more alcohol, and so on. There are some warning signs you can watch out for to understand whether alcohol is affecting your mood or not. These warning signs include feeling tired because of a hangover, feeling low, not getting sufficient sleep after drinking, and experiencing elevated levels of anxiety in situations you normally are comfortable in.

Family Life

Alcohol abuse and alcoholism not only affects your health, but it also affects your family life. There is a direct relationship between alcohol problems and relationship struggles. Alcoholism and alcohol abuse can lead to poor communication between partners, domestic violence, interpersonal conflict, and the severing of all the important relationships in your life. It is not just you that experiences anxiety and depression, but even your loved ones will face the same. It is believed that the partners and spouses of alcoholics are at a greater risk of experiencing stress-related health issues.

The harmful effect of alcohol is not just restricted to your intimate relationships. For instance, children also suffer when they have a parent with alcohol problems. It places stress on the parent-child bond, increases exposure of a child to parental conflict, and the lack of adequate parental oversight might lead to the child ending up in risky situations. It also makes it quite difficult to maintain clear or consistent household rules and increases the risk of a child toward mental illness and exposure to violence. The chances of the biological child of an alcoholic parent developing alcoholism later in life are also quite high. The biological children of alcoholic women might suffer from fetal alcohol syndrome, alcohol-related neurodevelopmental disorder, alcohol-related congenital disabilities, or partial fetal alcohol syndrome. Each of these conditions tends to have a significant effect on the growth and development of the child, and they are incurable. So, the biological child of an alcoholic woman might end up with poor socialization skills, inability to focus, learning and memory difficulties, impulsive behavior, lack of emotion regulation, and decreased ability to go through their life effectively.

Social Behavior

The social effect of alcohol is another undeniable aspect of your life. All those under the influence of alcohol experience a decrease in their sense of inhibition.

Therefore, they are more impulsive and have a reduced chance of rationally considering the consequences of all their impulsive behaviors. It can lead to heightened levels of violence, participation in risky activities such as driving under the influence or engaging in unprotected sex, unplanned pregnancies, the risk for victimization via physical assault or sexual assault, accidental injuries and death, or even alcohol poisoning.

Alcohol dependence or alcohol use disorder can also cause trouble for you at work. For instance, it would be quite difficult to be productive at work if all your time is spent recovering from a hangover or thinking about the next drink you can have. Difficulty in concentration also reduces your overall productivity.

So, alcohol has an overall damaging effect on all aspects of your life, regardless of whether it is your emotional or physical wellbeing. After going through the list of all the harmful effects of alcohol discussed in this section, you might be a little worried. However, most of these damages can be easily reversed if you stop drinking and immediately get the help you need. You will learn more about all this in the subsequent chapters in this book.

Chapter 10: What Is Drug Classification?

Drug classifications are used to organize drugs into categories.

Classifying drugs by substance similarities is important because chemically similar drugs often have identical influences and risks. Someone dependent on a drug is likely to misuse it and be reliant on another drug that is chemically similar. Despite these generalities, chemically identical drugs may have different legal and medical effects.

Many people classify drugs according to their impact on the brain and body; for example, some drugs make a user vigorous and energetic while some produce a calmer feeling.

Most countries have a legal classification system for drugs. These systems determine the circumstances, if any, under which the drug is legal, various requirements for the medication, and any legal fines connected with ownership, distribution, or it's manufacturing. Legal classifications are often based on the therapeutic value of the drug and its identified risk.

There's a disagreement on how drugs ought to be classified, even among experts, meaning the same medication could be classified differently under two categories using the same name. Due to these disagreements, it's impossible to have a "definitive" band of drug classifications.

Drug Classifications Based on Chemical Makeup

Alcohol

Alcohols are the most abused element in the world, including in the U.S. Alcohols influence numerous body systems, which in turn causes many risks for users. Alcohol consumption produces emotions of euphoria and decreases inhibitions, and also causes vision impairment. Alcohols are a central anxious system depressant, it causes the most regrettable long-term injury to the liver. There are many forms of alcohol consumption which includes:

Beer.

Wine.

Liquor.

Opioids

Also called opiates, opioids are either created from the drug opium or are chemicals designed to mimic it. Opioids work by interacting with neurotransmitters in the heart and obstructs the signals they are sending. This enables opioids to serve as powerful pain killers, nonetheless, it could cause extreme pleasure, leading to addiction. Opioid addiction is one of the most serious problems faced in America today, they are the most addictive of all known chemicals, and they are also one of the deadliest. Some of the most well-known opioids include:

Heroin.

Fentanyl.

Oxycodone.

Benzodiazepines

Benzodiazepines, or Benzos, are a group of drugs that work by interacting with the neurotransmitter gamma-aminobutyric acid-A (GABA-A). Each Benzo interacts with GABA-A in various ways, which is why each Benzo effects the body and brain differently. Benzos are recommended to take care of different psychiatric and rest conditions; however, they are commonly abused. Benzos are highly addictive and may cause numerous medical and mental problems. Types of Benzos include:

Ativan.

Valium.

Xanax.

Cannabinoids

Cannabinoids are a group of drugs that are chemically similar to tetrahydrocannabinol (THC), the active agent in weed. Cannabinoids create emotions of happiness, however, they adversely affect mental and physical health. Cannabinoids are the most commonly abused drugs after alcohol, and they are increasingly getting legal approval. Although considered less addictive than other drug classifications, cannabinoids can significantly harm a person's mental and physical health. Types of cannabinoids include:

Marijuana.

Hashish.

Barbiturates

Barbiturates slow down the work of the central nervous system; they are derivatives from the substance barbituric acidity. Barbiturates were historically popular for treating psychiatric and sleep issues, anesthesia and other conditions such as epilepsy and headache. Barbiturates are highly addictive, and they have a high potential of overdose risk because they might cause several systems in the body to shut down.

Types of barbiturates include:

Amytal.

Luminal.

Pentobarbital.

Classification of Drugs based on Effects

Depressants

More commonly referred to as "downers," depressants create emotions of relaxation and tiredness. Even though many serve legitimate purposes like fighting mental disorder and sleeplessness, these are commonly abused because they may also evoke emotions of euphoria. Depressants aren't only one of the highly addictive drugs; they are also one of the most highly dangerous and most likely to cause an overdose. Types of depressants include:

Alcohol.

Opiates.

Barbiturates.

Stimulants

Also known as "uppers," the first use of stimulants is to improve energy, concentration, and alertness. Stimulants are believed to produce a rush i.e high energy. For some time, stimulants are believed to improve efficiency and performance, while evoking pleasure. Over time, stimulants are incredibly addictive and possess a very high prospect of abuse. Types of stimulants include:

Adderall.

Cocaine.

Meth.

Hallucinogens

Hallucinogens sometimes referred to as dissociative, affect the user's knowledge of reality, often resulting in auditory and visual hallucinations, which is referred to as "tripping." Although hallucinogens are often less addictive than other drug classifications, their immediate effects are usually more serious and dangerous. Types of hallucinogens include:

LSD.

Psilocybin Mushrooms.

PCP.

Inhalants

Inhalants are a large collection of chemicals that are ingested mainly by breathing them in or huffing. Most inhalants are used materials that are in no way fit for human consumption. Since there's a wide range of inhalants, most produce feelings of increased energy. Inhalants are less studied than other drugs; while they tend to be less addictive when compared to other substances, the use of inhalants is dangerous and causes many serious health effects. Types of commonly abused inhalants include:

Paint thinner.

Toenail polish remover.

Gasoline

The Federal government passed the Controlled Chemicals Do something in 1970 in response to the drug epidemic. This work established five drug classifications. What use a drug is put to dependent upon the legitimacy and it's potential medical uses, combined with the prospects of abuse and the risk of addiction. America must classify the use of certain drugs using schedules to stick to diplomatic agreements, like the Single Convention on Narcotic Drugs.

Schedule V

Program V drugs have the fewest regulations and most affordable fines of any drug classification. Plan V drugs have the best accepted medical purpose, and a lesser prospect of abuse than Timetable IV drugs, and possess a lesser prospect of addiction than Schedule IV drugs. For instance:

Lomotil.

Motoren.

Lyrica

Schedule IV

Plan IV drugs have regulations and fines among the Timetable V and Routine III drugs. Plan IV drugs have the best accepted medical purpose; a minimal prospect of misuse; and a minimum potential of cravings. For instance:

Ambien.

Darvocet.

Tramadol

Schedule III

Schedule III drugs have more regulations and stricter fines than Regular IV drugs and fewer rules and less severe penalties than Plan II drugs. Schedule III drugs have the best medical use; a smaller potential of misuse than Regimen I and II drugs; and a low prospect of addiction. Types of Plan III drugs include:

Anabolic steroids.

Ketamine.

Vicodin.

Schedule II

Schedule II drugs have more regulations and harsher fines than any other drug aside from the Regular We drugs. Plan II drugs have the best medical use, a high potential of misuse, and a severe dependence risk. Types of Timetable II drugs include:

Codeine.

Methadone.

Ritalin.

Schedule I

Drugs in this category have more rules and stricter fines than any other drugs. The program I drugs don't have any reputable accepted medical use and an increased prospect of abuse. Types of medications in Timetable I include:

Ecstasy.

Quaaludes.

Don't Let Drugs Ruin Your Life

It doesn't matter whether you or someone you love is dependent on a Routine V benzodiazepine or an opioid. Dependency can be a terrible condition; it prevents you from living the life you ought to live. While all drug classifications will require special treatment, some rehabs could help. Consult experts in the field to discover the best treatment option for you.

Understanding Illegal Drugs

Illicit-drugs refer to highly addictive and unlawful drugs such as heroin, marijuana, and meth. Your choice of drug is usually a voluntary one, however, quitting after becoming addicted can be very difficult.

Drug dependency affects a person's mental health; how they perceive and understand things; and can also modify their behavior and character.

The beginning of drug disorder is marked by a physical dependency on it, tolerance to the drug, and the effects of its misuse. Tolerance occurs if you take more of the drug to obtain the same results as when you began. When the user is exposed to certain truths about the drug, there might be a relapse if their attempt to quit. However, there is a desire to avoid using the drug, as well as prioritizing its use over relationships and family obligations.

Drawback symptoms are severe they may include chest palpitations and seizures depending on the kind of drug used. Drug disorder enforces a psychological reliance on the substance, which means that the user needs the drug to be in the right frame of mind.

When a person experiencing drug disorder realizes the negative effects of their drug use, they start to struggle to live off it. The best way to overcome dependency on illegal drugs is treatment at an inpatient rehabilitation center.

At an inpatient rehabilitation center, medical doctors work carefully with recovering patients to diagnose the cause of their substance abuse, such as any reoccurring mental health disorders. During rehab, patients learn healthy and productive ways that do not only help them to stay off drugs but also help them to remain happy and live a pleasing and fulfilling life.

Types of illegal Drugs

If you or someone you know is fighting a drug disorder, you're not alone in. About 23.9 million people in America aged 12 or older - approximately 9.2% of the population - had used illegal drugs months before the study in 2012. Rates of illegal drug use are highest among those aged 18 to 25.

The most frequent types of illegal drugs used are:

Cocaine

Cocaine is a powerful addictive stimulant produced from the leaves of the South American Coca herb and usually comes in powder form. Street names for cocaine include blow, bump, coke, and snow. Cocaine is mainly sniffed or injected, and could also be smoked or administered on the skin.

Crack Cocaine

Crack is the purer and potent version of cocaine, which comes in blocks or crystals. Split cocaine is usually smoked and gets to the brain faster and result in a short-lived - yet extreme energy. Also, it is commonly injected.

Ecstasy

Used by many high-schoolers and adults, it is a party or rave medicine. Its psychoactive results include high sensory notions and may cause reduced inhibition. Ecstasy is taken in pill form or dissolved in water, but can also be snorted or injected.

Hallucinogens

LSD, PCP, mushrooms, and salvias are types of psychoactive or mind-changing drugs; while dependant on this drug is less common than other drugs, the use and abuse of the drug could cause adverse effects.

Heroin

Heroin is a highly addictive compound that is gotten from the opium poppy flower. It is available in a white-brownish powder, or as a dark and sticky element referred to as "dark tar." Heroin is mainly injected, though it can also be snorted, smoked, or swallowed.

Inhalants

Inhalants include household items such as spray paints, markers, and cleaning supplies that are inhaled through the mouth or nose to feel high or energized. Inhaling certain types of chemicals can lead to heart failure and ultimately death.

Ketamine

It is medically used as an anesthetic in veterinary practice. When abused, ketamine could cause hallucinations, sedation, and confusion.

Marijuana

Cannabis is one of the most abused illegal drugs.

The main psychoactive ingredient, THC, causes short-term euphoria, accompanied by drowsiness, slowed response time, and excessive hunger.

Meth

Meth is an extremely dangerous stimulant that may cause users to become instantly addicted. The short-term effects of meth consist of alertness and euphoria. However, long-term usage of meth can lead to problems such as violent behavior, severe dental hygiene problems, psychosis, and severe paranoia.

Synthetic Marijuana

Synthetic marijuana recognizes a growing level of manufactured substances that contain a chemical material exactly like THC. Although human-made marijuana is promoted like a legal option, the substance's results could be unstable and more extreme than its natural counterpart.

Illegal Drug Results and Abuse

Many illegal drugs pose serious health threats, even though taken in small doses. Some drugs could cause dependency after use. People who become reliant on illegal drugs are at a greater risk of overdose, which might be fatal. Many overdoses happens each time a person relapses after wanting to quit. They think they need the same treatment as before, forgetting their body is used to the number of drugs they take. That's the problem for those who take illegal drugs through injection.

Heroin is a drug that poses a threat of relapse and overdose. Unfortunately, the number of fatalities linked to heroin and other opioids has substantially increased in the last decade. From 2002 to 2017, the quantity of opioid-related deaths grew more than four times.

Repeated use of illegal substances can make the user vulnerable to short and long term consequences. Excessive drug use can cause damage to your brain and may disrupt your psychological well-being. This might make a person behave abnormally and cause them to make self-destructive decisions such as driving when high.

There are various ways illegal drugs can negatively affect a person:

Damages to relationships with spouses, family members, and friends.

Problems carrying out daily and social responsibilities.

Lateness to work or avoiding going to work because of drugs.

Lack of motivation to make good grades in school.

Financial hardships due to spending money to keep a drug habit.

Legal effects, such as being arrested for drugs.

Treatment of Illegal Drug Addiction

If someone you know is fighting illegal substance abuse, you will find multiple options for treatment and recovery. Whether you choose inpatient or outpatient treatment, finding a rehabilitation center may be the basic step to recover from drug abuse disorder. Learn about treatment plans for your specific needs.

What is Overdose?

An overdose is a biological response your body gives when it receives a lot of substance or combination of chemicals. An overdose could be intentional or accidental. People can overdose on illegal drugs, alcohol, prescribed medications, and many other substances. Often, overdoses are fatal, however, a lot of people who have overdosed could be saved if treatment is provided immediately. Overdose happens to be the leading cause of many accidental deaths in America. In the case of drugs, there are various ways your body could become overwhelmed by substances. However, the most frequent cause of death of any chemical overdose is respiratory failure.

Depressant Overdose

Depressants that affect the central nervous system (CNS), include opioids, benzodiazepines, and alcohol consumption. Drugs that are CNS depressants lower blood pressure and body temperature; slows heartbeat and breathing. That's the reason these drugs cause sedative effects, which result in anxiety and an increase in calm and ecstatic effect. When an excessive amount of depressants is used, it could result in adverse effects, such as respiratory failure, overdose, coma, and even death

Opioid Overdose

Opioids are one of the natural drugs to overdose on, given how they react when taken. Your body provides opioid receptors in different areas, in the brain, central and peripheral nervous systems, as well as the gastrointestinal tract. When someone uses opioids, these receptors are activated and slow the body down. Whenever your body becomes overwhelmed by opioids, several receptors are blocked, and it can't perform other functions. This will result in a higher risk of overdosing, which can decelerate a person's breathing. Different opioids may be severe, where it could take minutes for a person who took heroin to experience the consequences from the overdose, someone who uses fentanyl will feel it within minutes. These powerful opioids are the reason the President of America declared a national opioid epidemic in 2017.

What is Naloxone?

Naloxone is an essential weapon in the fight against opioid overdose, Naloxone popularly made from Narcan, is an opioid antagonist that will stop the effects of opioids on the body. If someone takes an overdose, and the condition is severe, several doses of Narcan can stop the severity, and save the person's life. Narcan is available without prescription in America.

Alcohol Overdose

An alcohol overdose happens when you drink more alcohol than your body can safely process. Generally, the body can process around one unit of alcohol each hour (approximated to be the amount of alcohol in a shot of liquor, a half-pint of beer, or 1 glass of wine).

If a person drinks more alcohol than this within a short while, the alcohol accumulates in the body because the body cannot metabolize the alcohol fast enough, and a build-up of alcohol spreads throughout your body. This may result in alcohol overdose referred to as alcohol poisoning.

Symptoms of alcohol poisoning include:

Mental confusion.

Vomiting.

Seizures.

Slow breathing.

Irregular breathing.

Hypothermia, bluish epidermis, paleness

Factors that influence your risk of having an alcohol overdose include:

Age.

Gender.

Body Size.

Tolerance.

Binge Drinking

Drug Use

Other medical issues

Additional risks that can occur due to drinking more amounts of alcohol than the body can metabolize are:

Slower breathing, gag reflex, and decreased heartbeat.

Cardiac arrest attributed to a decrease in body temperature (hypothermia).

constant seizures attributed to low blood sugar

Stimulant Overdose.

Stimulants, such as meth or cocaine, concentrate on the CNS, however, on the other hand, opioids increase heartbeat, blood circulation pressure, body temperature, and breathe. A stimulant overdose occurs when the heart, the respiratory system, or blood circulation system is overworked to a point of wearing down.

Symptoms of stimulant overdose include:

Jerking or stiff limbs.

Rapid increase in body temperature or a sudden outburst of high fever.

Increasing pulse.

Loss of consciousness.

Seizures or convulsions.

Chest pain.

Severe headaches.

Excessive sweating.

Irritability and agitation.

Disorientation or mental confusion.

Severe hypertension.

Delirium.

Stroke.

Cardiac arrest.

Cardiovascular arrest.

Abnormal or shallow breathing

Some medications can help reduce or stabilize symptoms, such as blood pressure, pulse, body temperature, and any respiratory disorder. There are also medications you could use to help someone who experiences convulsions or seizures, such as anti-epileptic medications. Getting the person to the nearest hospital as soon as you can help save a life.

Getting Help for Overdose

Remember that treating overdose at home won't be the same as getting help from a hospital. Even if the patient seems to have recuperated, there is still a chance that a relapse might occur or that something is going on in the body the patient is not aware of. Taking the patient to a hospital will make a lot of difference in whether the patient will survive or die.

Overdose is a frightening term, it is often associated with death, however, it doesn't always lead to it. Life continues after treatment from an overdose, but the patient must understand the concept and learn from it.

Recovery isn't something that is accomplished quickly, however, it's possible, and not only that, there's also a guarantee that the patient might never suffer an overdose again.

If you don't know how to go about it, or you need help for someone you love, please speak to a treatment specialist. They're there, 24/7 to answer any questions you may have, whether it's for yourself or someone else.

Chapter 11: Self-Trust

Have you ever noticed how in the morning, you're fully able to decide that you'll have nothing to drink tonight, then by 5:00, the anxiety starts to sink in, and before you know it, you can't even fathom the idea of having a dry evening? Examining the reason for things like this is key in recognizing the power your ego has over your important decisions. How, in the morning, your better sensibilities seem to be in control, and as the day moves along, they steadily give way to the overwhelming drive of the ego.

The ego is like a child, conditioned to be satiated by what it's used to, and in return, reward you with a drip of dopamine, the chemical utilized by the brain's built-in "reward system." The child cries and cries until you give it it's lollipop. This is the basis of how not only problem drinking, but all bad habits, are created and sustained; from simple thumb-sucking as an infant, to drug use as an adult.

The crying is silent. It comes in the form of anxiety. Of boredom. Of unhappiness. With you, completely under the influence of your ego, not even conscious of your ego to begin with, all you can do to stop your self-destructive behavior is to sit and suffer through it. The pangs of anxiety. The rationalization creeping into your mind, trying to convince yourself to take the drug. The boredom. The malaise. And who can manage this struggle of will power indefinitely? Not many. This is why at least one alcoholic died in the time it took you to read this paragraph. A grotesque, undignified death.

It is certainly the right decision to quit drinking. Quitting drinking is, without a doubt, the correct decision to make, just as the right decision for Sandy is certainly to eat less and exercise more. Yet the ego stands in our way. To be owned by the ego is to make these unquestionably bad decisions. To live from inside the ego means to be constantly under its power, no matter whether it wants booze, cake, cigarettes, submarine sandwiches, or anything else; whatever you've gotten it used to. So, how do we get outside of it?

The following is an excerpt from an article from psychologytoday.com, by Marc Lewis Ph.D., entitled: Addicted Brains: The Key to Quitting: Self-Trust Part 1, Ego Depletion. Addicts have a hard time trusting themselves after so many failures, Nov 14, 2013.

"A few months ago I realized that I had something important to say to addicts who wanted to quit but hadn't yet figured out how. I was invited to participate in a TEDx event on the theme of trust. For me that meant trust and addiction. Hmmmm....what could I say about that?

That nobody trusts an addict? Not exactly news... That addicts can't trust the treatment industry? Ho hum. Then it hit me: The crucial role of "self-trust" in recovery. That's what worked for me, 32 years ago, when I finally broke my psychological dependence on opiates. Mightn't it work for others?

I had promised myself I was finished with drugs many times before, and I'd fallen off the wagon just as many. As is typical of addicts. Roughly 200 times in four years, and this yo-yo routine was killing me. Then, one time, something changed in the way I said it to myself. Instead of saying "only on weekends" or "just no injecting," I said "never again." And this time I trusted it. Suddenly I felt a new kind of warmth, engaging, kind, and smart. Instead of saying "sure, I've heard that before", a higher self (or at least a sense of self that extended into the future) put its arm around me and said: "we" are going to make it this time. We are that strong.

But why was it so difficult until then? Why is it so hard for addicts to "just say no?" We can answer this question only if we can explain what it is about addiction that works against self-trust.

There are two psychological phenomena that are central. I'll talk about one of them now and save the other for my next post.

Ego depletion refers to our fundamental inability to maintain impulse control for a long period of time.

Areas of prefrontal cortex (dorsolateral PFC and anterior cingulate) that are in charge of self-control run out of fuel. Like muscles, these areas get weakened and strained with continuous use. So, you can maintain self-control for a while—but not for very long.

In a classic experiment by psychologist Roy Baumeister, subjects come to the lab hungry. They are told not to eat either from a bowl of chocolate chip cookies (one group) or a bowl of radishes (the other group) sitting right in front of them. After several minutes, they have to complete cognitive tasks requiring self-control. Those who had to suppress their impulse to eat the cookies did less well on those tasks. (Nobody had a strong impulse to eat the radishes.) They had used up some of that precious cognitive resource— inhibitory control.

Ego depletion is a serious problem for addicts of all stripes: because the thing you're trying to control is there all the time. The bar on the corner, the phone number of your dealer, the bottle in the medicine chest—cues associated with your addiction are always present.

And addicts have to control their impulses, not just for minutes, but for hours, day after day, week after week. So, they run out of capacity, and they give in.

Recent research shows that people who believe in their capacity for self-control are less affected by ego depletion. Why should this be? How can a subjective state, a feeling, have such influence on a fundamental brain mechanism?

I think it's because, if you don't believe you can do it, the task is actually two tasks. You have to control not only the impulse but also your own doubt. Trying to maintain that double inhibition, to maintain your confidence while controlling your actions...exhausts your resources all the sooner.

That makes it very tough for addicts. Why should they trust their impulse control? They've failed time after time. So, each time, ego depletion is like a poison just waiting to take effect. And each time they fail, their capacity for self-trust is further weakened. All their trust is eventually invested in the drug, drink, or behavior they've come to rely on. And that ends up betraying them as well.

I'm always struck by a certain irony: People think addicts are weak and lazy. In fact it's the opposite. Addicts work harder than anyone else at keeping things together.

The second phenomenon is delay discounting. That's the tendency to devalue long-term rewards in favor of immediate rewards. Which happens to be an unfortunate side effect of dopamine's impact on attention and motivation. Dopamine metabolism is the so-called common pathway to addiction.

For now, let's just say that ego depletion and self-trust are mutually incompatible. Which means that ego depletion loses its insidious power to sabotage you when you finally figure out how to trust yourself. You don't have to grit your teeth and say "no" over and over if you actually believe in your own resolve. And that moment, when you switch sides and become your own coach, feels so right...that you already know it's going to work before the first day is over."

Let's read that last sentence again: "And that moment, when you switch sides and become your own coach, feels so right... that you already know it's going to work before the first day is over."

This is the truth, and let that be a great encouragement to you. I remember the moment this actually happened to me, and I'll discuss it a little later.

Self-trust is a good way to describe what I'll be helping you develop in this book. With the ego in the way, self-trust is more of a fanciful idea than a real-life goal for an addict. But in the most practical terms I can, I'm going to show you how to make this principle a part of your new foundation. Teaching you how to exercise this principle is the main point of this book. The concept of "switching sides and becoming your own coach" is exactly the solution to following your own good advice; the same good advice you'd give to anyone else you cared about. The advice you just can't seem to follow yourself for some reason. But how to do it? Once we understand what's standing in the way, I'll be able to walk you through it.

When you have that pang of anxiety on Sunday night that you have to go to work the next morning, it comes from the ego. When you just have to smoke that cigarette despite your respiratory infection, it's the ego. When you need a drink, despite all your better sensibilities, whether you need to get up early in the morning, whether you're on antibiotics and have been told not to drink, whether you have the flu, and might very well puke it right back up, or whether your eyes are yellowing from a failing liver; it's the ego.

As I've explained, the ego wants what it's used to. It understands no consequences. It is devoid of all reason. These things simply aren't part of its job description.

The ego is a rather imperfect mechanism of our personality. It might compel us to change to another lane when a tailgating vehicle creeps up behind us—certainly a good thing. It might lead us across the street to avoid a suspicious-looking character—also a good thing. It might ask us to do questionable things also, depending on our habits, like go to the gym when our muscles are already sore, or put in some extra overtime at the expense of family-time. The point is, the ego is a creature of habit, and for most people, sits in the driver seat of our personality-mobiles, driving us this way and that with a simple, incredibly effective steering mechanism. This way is rewarded with the excretion of a little dopamine, causing a sensation that you've done something good, and the other way, leading to a sense of dissatisfaction, making you feel like you've done something bad. For most of us, bought and paid-for completely by our egos, this mechanism runs our lives so powerfully, it undermines our entire right to free-will. Sure, we have the free-will to do as we choose, but at the risk of being penalized by our own precious brain-chemistry, deprived of the very impulses that gives us the will to go on in the first place. No fair, right? You got it.

But you are not without recourse.

Established Fact:

Our egos are ever-present; will power alone is a feeble defense against it. Self-trust is key.

Chapter 12: Addiction

People often find their way to recovery in the midst of a crisis. Someone standing at the crossroads of recovery, may have been arrested for DUI, may have been fired, or may have received a scary report from the doctor. He may have heard the bottom line demand from his spouse: "Get help or we are getting a divorce." Or, the alcoholic/addict may in fact, have a moment of clarity and really be able to see that he does have a problem and that help and abstinence are called for. The alcoholic/addict feels afraid. He feels ashamed. He feels angry at others or at himself for being in this position in the first place.

Fear, coercion or crisis helps him find his way into recovery. Fear is a fairly good short term motivator, but not so good in the long run. Once the fear subsides and the crisis is over, it is very easy to lose your motivation and momentum. At the point where the cycle of addiction is interrupted by failing to take the next drink, dose, or joint, there is a lot of tension, anxiety, and mindfulness of where you are in the process. Detox or withdrawal may occur, with physical and/or emotional symptoms being very consciously experienced.

When you get to feeling better physically and emotionally after detoxing, it is easy to lose your momentum. Your focus on recovery can dissolve. Some of the problems that once motivated your recovery might be resolved now. Because you have quit drinking or using, your spouse and kids are once again speaking to you and are in the process of forgiving you. You may have even won back some trust. Everything seems to be going well.

Under these circumstances it isquite easy for you to take your eyes off the target and lose your focus on recovery. Erroneously, you may believe that your abstinence is not so fragile now. Feeling better, you may think you have it "whipped".

Without actively focusing on your continuing abstinence and recovery, your behavior can begin to drift away from the newly instituted behavioral changes that you have made. You run the risk of returning to old thinking, old feelings, and then ultimately old behavior. The reason why this would happen is that you are not consciously taking steps to continue on a path of recovery. This path involves many changes in your behavior and in your life style. Without making conscious choices in regard to how each decision affects your new recovery life or your old addiction life, you are unconsciously choosing your old life. Choosing recovery is not like jump starting your damaged car battery where once you get it started, it recharges itself as run it. You have to continuously work a program of recovery. Without doing so, your efforts will be short-lived.

You will quit going to counseling. You will quit going to meetings. You will have stopped calling your recovery support people. Your defenses will go back up and you may take exception to the feedback of significant others who tell you that you are acting like you used to before recovery.

You won't be able to see that you are on the road to relapse. You won't be able to understand why they are concerned. You won't be able to identify the behavioral changes that scare them because you will be back in denial. Being around old drinking/using environments and friends don't scare you. You can't understand why it would scare your significant others. After all, you told them that you are not going to relapse. You have learned your lesson. What more do they want?

After awhile, you will begin to think that you have your drinking or using under control now. When you think of addiction as a thing of the past, that you now have it under control, you will begin to entertain the notion that you can now drink or use without negative consequences.If any of this sounds like your recent experience, you are in big trouble. You are in the relapse process and unless you do something now, you will relapse--and soon.

Addiction recovery is a lifelong process, just as recovery from all chronic diseases are. To empower yourself and your addicted loved one, gain as many tools and resources as you can. My website has a number of individual and family dynamics of addiction and recovery

Addiction and Recovery - Maintaining

The decision to confront an alcoholic is never an easy one to make. The most important thing is you should never attempt it when the alcoholic is currently under the influence of alcohol. The confrontation should be planned when he or she is sober. Confronting an alcoholic is sometimes called an intervention and must be carefully planned according to recommended expert guidelines, preferably those issued by a knowledgeable organization like Al-Anon which is the support group for family members of alcoholics. Also, prior to confronting an alcoholic, you should check with the person's doctor or a specialist in treating alcoholic disorders to determine how to prepare yourself and any others who might be helping you to confront a drinker about whom you are concerned. We have listed nine tips that may be helpful in preparing for an intervention.

Instead of formulating a confrontation plan on your own, see what the experts advise by talking to the Al-Anon association in your area. People there can advise you how to plan the intervention, and provide useful resources and information, too. If Al-Anon is unavailable in your area, make an appointment with a licensed therapist, counselor, or psychologist to discuss the nature of the problem and how it might best be approached. Although confronting an alcoholic can be similar in many respects for many families, it is a good idea to clarify unique circumstances or personal characteristics that could make a difference on the outcome.

You might find yourself wanting to berate and condemn a loved one should they come home intoxicated yet again. This fails to be productive as the drunk will ignore the criticism while under the alcohol influence and most likely forget about it the following when day when sober. It is crucial to talk to the person when sober and with a bit of luck, open to the idea of hearing your concerns. If a spontaneous opening should not happen, try to

151

schedule a talk after dinner or when the two of you have some privacy and cannot be interrupted.

Other relatives, close friends, or even members of Al-Anon that you may have met can by your supporters, as they may have been in comparable situations as you at some point. They may even decide to join you in confronting the alcoholic in your family. That decision can depend on you and the circumstances involving the person who drinks too much, as well as professional opinions about the situation.

When the times comes to confront the alcoholic, you must not be wishy-washy or indirect. Use a factual tone of voice and lay out the situation. Use examples of the drunkard's problem behavior and ensuing results. List dates, frequency of bad behavior, amounts of alcohol consumed or sums of money spent on drinking, and other data to support your claims. Please note that it takes courage to confront an alcoholic, so don't back down. If the alcoholic chooses to argue with you, remain calm and point to the facts.

An alcoholic often learns how to sidestep responsibility and manipulate other people to disregard his misdeeds or cover for him at work or in public in order to continue his habits. If you find yourself enabling the drinking, the alcoholic may presume he can have his way again to get out of the intervention without making any changes. Part of an intervention's impending success lies in the family member who leads it being able to change also. Ending the cycles that support the alcoholic's drinking is essential in helping them overcome their problem. Never allow the alcoholic to defeat what you are trying to accomplish.

Coupled with confronting an alcoholic with the consequences of his behavior is the need for a plan of recovery. If you are working with Alcoholics Anonymous or Al-

Anon, they can help you with making arrangements for a problem drinker to enter a rehabilitation program, either onsite at a facility for this purpose, or as an outpatient in a local clinic or support group. In some cases, a halfway house might be an appropriate alternative. Find out ahead of time if a particular detoxification program will accept the problem drinker you are working with, and make preliminary arrangements for the person to be admitted immediately following the intervention. Make it clear that you cannot guarantee the drinker will enroll, much less stay with the program, unless he accepts the program as part of his new life of abstaining from drink.

If the alcoholic agrees to go into rehab, family members should try to provide support and encouragement during the detoxification phase and rehabilitation program, which involves patient and family education and can last anywhere between several days to several months.

Most programs last 28 days or less, given people's job and family responsibilities, and some of the rehabilitators can continue as a non-resident while resuming career and household duties. However the program plays out, love, acceptance, and willingness to support changes in lifestyle can go a long way toward helping the alcoholic become successful in rehabilitation.

As mentioned briefly above, family members living with an alcoholic must be willing to take responsibility for their behavior and make necessary changes, too. Adjustments might include refusing to cover for an alcoholic's inability to go to work by reporting him absent, paying bills that the drinker should pay when he has spent his paycheck for alcoholic beverages, and letting the drunkard abuse or terrorize the family by acts of recklessness or violence. Sobriety can actually make life harder for the drinker and his family as everyone adjusts to new rules and learns how to follow through consistently. Some ex-drinkers can be ill-tempered, demanding, and peevish, while others may act guilty, embarrassed, or repentant.

After confronting an alcoholic, results may not appear automatically. The drinker may vacillate between agreeing to rehab and resisting it, or he may enter rehab but leave early or fall off the wagon after completing the program. Nothing is guaranteed. After confronting an alcoholic, all you can do is continue to hold your line and wait for the drinker's response. That alone will determine the outcome of your intervention. If the drinker opts not to continue treatment or it proves unsuccessful, the family should continue to receive counseling and support as they make decisions about the future.

One of the most difficult things is to live with an alcoholic. Their inability to control their drinking creates problems for not only themselves but for everyone around them. It can be hard for family to separate themselves from the drinker and create effective boundaries against the alcoholic in order to prevent the drinker's problems from spreading. With knowledge, professional support, and loads of assurance, relatives can incorporate a dose of tough love into their confrontation to give that person a chance at recovery. An intervention is a positive step in the right direction, a direction that includes admitting a problem and choosing to have the willingness to take action to end the addiction. These steps will lead to a better life for both the drinker and those he loves.

Stop Addiction

How you can stop addiction, and stop letting drugs control your life.

You have no control of your life when addicted to drugs, and YES, alcohol IS a drug, although you may think that you are totally in control. Stop addiction? "One might say." I've got no addiction to stop.

Possibly you are thinking:

I work at a good job making a decent salary.

I have a home, and a family I am supporting.

I am not standing on a street corner begging for money and then buy drugs or maybe a bottle of booze.

Well, here's the hardcore truth...

Just because you are a functioning addict does not mean there isn't a problem there. If you have to have a drink or even a glass of wine, or any mind altering drug just to have fun or socialize. If you get up in the morning and you have to do drugs in order to make it through your workday.

Then no, you are NOT in control of your life and there are issues to address.

You are just like other addicts who actually know they are addicts and feel trapped in their addiction seeing no way out.

Addicts need drugs just to function or to have fun. It doesn't matter where we come from or what drugs we do or have done, or how good of a job we have. Addiction can happen to anyone.

Are you wondering who I am and how I know about these things?

I am a 47-year-old recovering drug addict. Drugs and alcohol had control of my life for 31 of those years. I was flying high on autopilot, in the self-destruction mode, and I found recovery just in time to save my life.

I have been clean and sober for almost four-and-a-half years now. Drugs and alcohol put me through a life of pain and survival through many traumatic events. In addition, I was in and out of jail more times than I can remember. Drugs and alcohol no longer control my life. I am living proof that recovery is possible for anyone who truly wants it. And I am living a life that I never thought would ever be possible.

I am now a published author and I have a future, without drugs. I escaped that trap and now I am living, not just existing. I lived in hell most of my life but I clawed my way out. And I want to share with anyone who cares to listen, how I got clean and have been able to remain so.

Believe me when I say, drugs do control your thinking. For example; they control who we think our friends are. In our addiction, our friends are people we only hang out with in bars, or that we sell drugs to, or buy drugs from. They are people who would sell their mother in order to get drugs. They are people we would have nothing to do with if we weren't addicted to drugs. Drugs also control what kind of jobs we can get because when applying for a job most jobs do drug and alcohol testing before they will hire you. Most of us have criminal records that keep us from getting the jobs we want. Drugs and alcohol make us lie, cheat and steal. The list goes on and on.

In my addiction I felt trapped, I did not know how to survive without drugs. This reality was just an illusion. I only felt trapped because I knew no other way to live. I didn't know how to put my hand out and ask for help. In my recovery however, I learned that we do have choices, and we do have the freedom to choose. Do we want to live? Or do we just want to exist and endure the painful life that we get from our addiction? There is a way to get out of the trap and stop addiction from controlling our lives.

If you have a problem with drugs and, or alcohol, and your feeling trapped in your addiction, I would like to give you some advice that worked for me and has proven to be very effective for millions of people to stop addiction and learn a new and wonderful way of living.

First of all, we must realize that we have a problem. Then realize that we cannot do this alone. For some of us, like myself, it is necessary to go into a residential drug rehabilitation program to get clean and continue recovery with 12-step meetings after we graduate. It is very important that when we decide we want to recover that we must go to 12-step meetings regularly. This is where we start to learn a new way to live and also learn that we are not alone.

We start making new friends, we learn that we must break all ties with our "friends" that use or drink. Please don't fool yourself into thinking you can hang around "friends" who are still using or drinking and not have it cause you to pick up. This is just another illusion; it will be just a matter of time before you are using or drinking again. If you have decided that you want recovery and your "friends" do not feel the same way. You must stay away from them for your own protection and recovery. It is important to put recovery first above everything. If they are truly your friends they will be happy for you and will understand. Once they see how much your life is changing for the better they just might join you on your road to recovery.

However, if they get mad at you for your decision, and try to get you to have a drink or indulge in some drugs with them, then they do not have your best interests at heart and you will surely know that they were never your friends to begin with.

I have met some of the best people I know in recovery, and I have found friendships that will last a lifetime. I mean real friends that will be there for me no matter what. People who truly care about me, people just like myself who know where I'm coming from, and it will be the same way for you.

When you first start attending meetings you may feel a little uncomfortable. It is normal to feel this way but as you continue going to meetings, you will make new friends, and you will start looking forward to attending meetings. That is the way it is for most of us. If you continue going to meetings, do what is suggested, and don't pick up no matter what, your life will get better. Once you start hearing other people's stories you will realize you are not alone. We are all seeking the same thing. Freedom from active addiction. When I first got to the program I had trust issues. Most of my life in my addiction, I found myself trying to trust untrustworthy people and was convinced that I could not trust myself. In recovery however, I began healing from my trust issues and have since learned to trust again. You will begin testing relationships with other recovering addicts and you just might be surprised at how easy it is to find good friends, people just like you who are not using. Recovery has been a lot of fun for me. We do many activities together. I was welcomed into a new family in recovery, and I get love and support from all of them.

After we go to a few meetings we find someone of the same gender who inspires us, we ask them to sponsor us as we begin working towards recovery. Don't be nervous about asking someone to sponsor you, when we sponsor someone it helps us as much as it helps the person who we sponsor. It is always an honor when a woman asks me to sponsor her. Many of us as we enter the program, have much pain and grief to get through. The 12-steps are the blueprints of our recovery. Our sponsor will guide us through working the steps. We learn a new way to live by applying spiritual principals to our daily lives. We learn to accept our past and let it go. As we begin our journey on our road to recovery we learn to live life on its own terms. We feel the pain, and we release it. We feel our feelings and we let them go. We heal from our past and move forward. Our lives become worthwhile and we lose the obsession to use. We move into our future and start living better lives.

If you have a problem with drugs and, or alcohol please get help and stop addiction from controlling your life. If you truly want to live a life free from active addiction. You can do it by making a decision and get into a 12-step program. Take back your life. Stop Addiction!

Chapter 13: How To Handle Cravings

One of the biggest hurdles you will have to overcome is how to handle your urge to drink, and how to avoid the cravings. The good news is that these urges are quite often very predictable and can thus be controlled. Figuring out what triggers your need to drink is the first part of the problem. Get a diary and write down each time a craving occurs. Soon you will be able to work out a pattern and discover exactly what, when and where these happen. Knowing this will help you to avoid them. For some people it's anger, for some it's sadness, and for some it's pure boredom that causes them to drink. Find your reason.

There are two types of triggers.

External triggers – these are situations, places, people and times of day that make you want to drink. Perhaps you normally meet work colleagues at the bar every day, or you routinely need a little drink after lunch. Do you perhaps have a certain friend that every time you see them you drink? These are the external triggers.

Internal triggers – these are a little harder to identify, as sometimes it's simply just a feeling and an urge that you suddenly want to drink. There will always be a reason for this but sometimes it just takes a bit of time and reflection to realize why. It could be a certain emotion that causes it, such as nervousness, excitement or sadness. It all boils down to figuring what that emotion is.

The art of distraction is possibly the best way to avoid a craving. Once you figure out when you get your cravings you can find ways to avoid caving in to this emotion, no matter how overwhelming it

168

may be. This is where distraction comes in. If you know an event is coming up that may cause a trigger, organize an activity for that time. Something that will keep you busy and help you forget the alcohol. You can't, of course, always know when a trigger is going to occur. So when it does, make sure you do something immediately to occupy your mind. Some ideas:

Phone or visit a friend.

Exercise. Whether this means a short walk around the block or a vigorous workout at the gym.

Play loud and uplifting music.

Clean. This may sound odd, but cleaning can sometimes be a very satisfying distraction, which leaves you with a feeling of achievement.

Play a game, read a book, watch a movie. Keep the mind occupied.

Create a schedule of activities, such as Tuesday is swimming, Wednesday going to visit a friend, Thursday going to see a play.

Meditation. Find a class nearby, Google meditation techniques or simply sit and meditate in your own way. Remember that you have used alcohol to relax for many years and now you need to learn to use other techniques to still your mind. Don't be frustrated and realize that it will take a lot of practice to get the stillness you desire. People without drinking problems battle with this so do not get unmotivated when you don't get it right the first time. If meditation alone doesn't work then try a yoga class, where you will learn meditation techniques through movement.

Remind yourself on why you gave up drinking in the first place. You need to learn to embrace your emotions, instead of masking them with alcohol. Remember that alcohol doesn't remove your problems; it only hides them for a small amount of time. Remind yourself that this only makes it worse. Tell yourself that you need to start facing your problems head on and dealing with them.

Acceptance. Be aware that urges will occur and simply wait until it passes.

Write a diary. Sometimes physically writing down your problems can make it go away. You can also use this as a motivation throughout your entire process and track your achievements along the way.

Write a blog. Even better than a diary because here you are sharing your experience with the world. Remember that you are not alone in this addiction and that other people are riding the same emotional rollercoaster as you are. Your blog might be just the thing they need to help them through this time. So use this blog to help not only yourself but also others. This is an incredibly rewarding process.

I'd like to take this time to congratulate you for coming this far into the process. Even just thinking about stopping is a step in the right direction. Remember why you are doing this. Even though the road may be hard and it may be long, you are creating a better life for yourself and those around you. Never look at your sobriety as unachievable. Rather look at it through manageable chunks. So right now commit to staying sober for one hour, move that to a few hours, move that to a day, to a week, to a month, to a year, to your life. Tell yourself that you are staying sober today, and then tomorrow say the same thing.

Chapter 14: Hire A Therapist

Therapy differs from all other forms of treatment because, with therapy, you are in the care of a professional. There are several types of therapy out there for dealing with alcoholism. I'm only going to cover cognitive-based therapy because it is by far the best.

Cognitive Behavioral Therapy(CBT) is based on the idea that behaviors and feelings are caused by thoughts and how one sees the world. That self-destructive behavior are not based on facts but instead originates from an individual past experiences in life, his learned beliefs and his fully developed coping mechanisms.

Its a therapy focused more on the thinking and the idea that even if you are unable to change your circumstances, you can change how you think about them and then behave.

CBT teaches how to find the connection between thoughts, feelings and actions and how this connection can impact recovery. It is widely used in addiction and other disorders such as eating disorder, attention deficit disorder, bipolar disorder, anxiety, and PTSD. CBT has been shown to be effective when used alone. However, according to the National Institute of Drug Abuse, CBT had been shown to work extremely well when combined with support groups and medications.

How it works

When you sign up for CBT, you are led to believe that many of your actions are unreasonable, and a lot of your thoughts and feelings originate not from facts but from past experiences and environmental factors.

It's important because if you understand why you feel the way you do and act in a certain way and how those influence your addiction. You are better equipped to overcome the impulsive behaviors, and plan your way out. Your therapist works with you to change your behavioral response to these negative thoughts and thereby stop the vicious cycle of binge drinking.

The very first step is recognizing your negative thoughts. Your negative thoughts are called "Automatic Negative thoughts" and they are often misconceptions due to your upbringing, and products of self-doubt and fear. These thoughts and the accompanying awful feelings are usually the cause of the clinical anxiety and depression. Which may be the source of your drinking problems since you are drinking to get rid of the negative thoughts and unpleasant feelings.

CBT focuses on both the thoughts and feelings that are driving your addiction and also on your reaction and instinctive behaviors. You are taught to examine your thoughts more carefully instead of just agreeing with them, changing the way you talk to yourself and then picking alternative behaviors each time you have an automatic thought.

In the treatment of alcohol addiction, the goals of CBT that you and your therapist work on includes;

Dismissing false beliefs that leads to binge drinking

Providing skill training to improve your moods

Planning time to engage in non-drug activities

Learning to recognize and avoid situations that can lead to alcohol abuse

Learning about internal and external triggers that lead to craving and binge drinking

Understanding what relapse is and how to cope with it.

CBT has two major components;

1. Functional analysis

Your therapist works with you to identify the thoughts, feelings, and circumstances leading to and following drinking. In time, you may find that the thoughts and feelings are due to some childhood abuse, long-held misconception or false memories and alcohol is just your coping mechanism.

You may equally find out that it's due to a long heard habit of beating yourself down every time you make a mistake or a misconception that you can't stay alone leading you to always seek out other's
-

companies. All these thoughts and more can lead to alcohol use disorder.

Functional analysis will help you know how you think, why you use drugs in the first place. The routes you take and the situations that can lead to relapse.

2. Skills training

The second step is learning better-thinking skills and how to react better to your thoughts. Your therapist helps you unlearn old habits and help you with developing new healthier skills and habits. You learn to talk better to yourself by praising yourself for the little gains and to motivate yourself better by considering the effects of drinking on your family. You learn new ways to cope with thoughts and circumstances that led to drinking in the past.

You are also taught specific behavioral techniques such as - talking back to automatic negative thoughts, not planning parties or visiting a bar if it makes you crave alcohol, choosing a different route for an evening stroll if it always takes you down to the bar, choosing a model in your neighborhood and then following their footsteps.

As you can see, CBT goes beyond just pouring your heart out to a listening therapist. It's a more goal-oriented therapy focused on short term problems. Your therapist and you work actively together on specific skill acquisitions to treat your addiction. And while other forms of therapy are less engaging and can take years. You will be done after taking 12-16 structured sessions spanning 60-90 days in planned rehabilitation programs.

CBT is also very adaptable meaning you can take your sessions from home or in an inpatient facility. The techniques can be performed at home, in the office or in a group setting.

The 12 step techniques

Cognitive-behavioral techniques are specific exercises aimed at thinking more accurately, managing triggers adequately and learning better behaviors. You'll often be taught several key techniques over 12 sessions.

Session 1 to 3

In the first three sessions, you will be taught to admit that a problem exists, acknowledging that it's difficult and seeking help. You will be guided through the defining the common thoughts and causes of your problems. The routines that lead to addiction and you will start learning skills to counter those thoughts and routines.

Session 4

Session four involves creating a catalog of all your negative thoughts, triggers, and impulsive behaviors, nothing that needs to be changed and then setting personal goals aimed at recovery and living a better life.

Session 5 to 7

These sessions encourage having an open relationship with your loved ones and honest communication in order to overcome your addiction. You talk things out with your therapist and you are urged to build relationships with supportive friends and family.

Session 8 to 10

These sessions teach you skills directed at improving your Current situation by addressing past mistakes and making the necessary amends. These sessions focus on reflecting on mistakes made during addiction and the negative experience your loved ones went through. You are urged to identify these mistakes, make the necessary amends and also address new mistakes.

Session 11 to 12

In the last sessions, you will be taught better coping mechanisms and empowering habits, and also sharing the experience with others. Sharing your experiences in private or in group sessions help you with the struggle and it strengthens your recovery.

Over the period of going through these sessions, you will be taught several psychological and social techniques that will aid your recovery. The key techniques include;

1. Thought examination

Usually, in depression and anxiety, your thoughts make no sense. There are usually patterns to these thoughts - you feel that you are bad, that you deserve bad things happening you and that bad things will always happen.

This makes no sense because nobody is born bad or fated to ill fate. But life experiences can lead you to develop several misconceptions that twist your reality. CBT teaches being mindful of your thoughts and then countering them with alcohol instead of drowning them in alcohol.

The goal is to list evidence for and against your thoughts and help you balance your thinking.

If you are fond of always drinking after work, your underlying thought maybe "I'm such a useless person with no skills, my manager is right to believe I have no skills, I should drink more to cope with my useless existence".

After examining the facts, that thought becomes " I do have skills, even if my manager can't recognize it now. I can always learn, heed his advice and learn from my mistakes, I don't need alcohol."

The more you compare the facts, with a cool head, the more you'll stop beating yourself down and can then choose better responses to your automatic thoughts that lead to better behaviors.

2. Visual based exposure

In this exercise, you are urged to frequently recall painful memories. Running from painful memories is a vicious cycle and the more you avoid them with alcohol, the larger they look over and overpower you.

Your CBT therapist urges you to think more about that memory that produces negative feelings. You are made to really expose yourself to the details - sight, sound, and emotions of the moment. It could be when you were abused as a kid or when you are bullied or made a nasty mistake.

By exposing yourself repeatedly to the negative memory, it loses its power over you and your anxiety reduces over time. It's a simple process that requires courage. Your therapist offers that courage. It works because fear is nothing but an illusion, the more you do what you fear, the more you overcome that fear.

3. Behavioral experiments

Behavioral therapist involves changing how you react to your negative thoughts and feelings to see which one drives change. Some people benefit more from self-kindness, forgiveness, and compassion. Others benefit from giving themselves some tough love and self-criticism. It's different for everyone. Your therapist works with you to employ the one that works for you.

4. Pleasant activity schedule

This involved making a list of fun and healthy activities to break up daily routines and counter impulsive behaviors. Rather than drinking when working, you are advised to take naps and listening to soothing music. You can play video games with your kids instead of partying it out with friends.

These tasks should be simple and easy to perform. And by scheduling them, you reduce your exposure to triggers and the subsequent urge to drink.

Chapter 15: How To Deal With

Withdraw Symptoms

Alcohol withdrawal refers to symptoms that may occur when a person who has been drinking too much alcohol on a regular basis suddenly stops drinking alcohol.

One justification that alcoholics will use for not giving up the abuse is their fear of alcohol withdrawals. The process of entering sober living can involve an uncomfortable few days, but the rewards that come afterward make it well worth it. The reality is that alcohol detox symptoms are rarely that uncomfortable and some people experience very little in the way of unpleasantness. The experience that the individual has with withdrawals can depend as much on their expectations as anything else.

Alcohol withdrawal symptoms usually occur within 8 hours after the last drink but can occur days later. Symptoms usually peak by 24 to 72 hours but may go on for weeks.

In symptoms you can find: anxiety, depression, fatigue, irritability, jumpiness, mood swings nightmares, not thinking clearly, among others.

People with moderate-to-severe symptoms of alcohol withdrawal may need inpatient treatment at a hospital or other facility that treats alcohol withdrawal. You will be watched closely for hallucinations and other signs of delirium tremens.

If you have mild-to-moderate alcohol withdrawal symptoms, you can often be treated in an outpatient setting. You will need someone to stay with you during this process who can keep an eye on you. You will likely need to make daily visits to your provider until you are stable.

Be patient. You cannot rush recovery. But you can go through it one day at a time. If you resent or attempt to speed up your way through it, you will become exhausted. And when you're exhausted you'll think of using alcohol to escape.

Practice self-care. Tell yourself, "What I'm doing is enough." Be good to yourself. That's what most addicts cannot do, and that's what you should learn in recovery. Recovery is the opposite of addiction.

Being able to relax will help you through this phase. When you are tense, you tend to dwell on your symptoms and make them worse. When you are relaxed, it is easier not to relapse.

Remember, every relapse, no matter how small, undoes the gains your brain made during recovery. Without abstinence, everything will fall apart. With abstinence everything is possible.

You will feel several things, above all, to return to the substance that your body needs. Be strong, never back down of you and your life again.

Conclusion

Thank you again for downloading this book!

I hope this book was able to give you some ideas and guidelines in order to stop drinking alcohol safely and effectively.

The next step is to put them into practice! Don't forget them. Think about the ideas I've presented in this book and choose the best for you. YOU CAN STOP DRINKING ALCOHOL. You just have to WANT IT.

Make your life better. Be the 1% of people who succeeds in life.

Take action TODAY!

Thank you again and good luck, my friend!

CPSIA information can be obtained
at www.ICGtesting.com
Printed in the USA
BVHW040258070521
606654BV00005B/631